D1766707

NICHOLAS S. DICAPRIO is Professor of Psychology at John Carroll University, and has a wide background in psychotherapy and research. Dr. DiCaprio has also formulated a new form of behavior therapy, Verbal Satiation Theory, and is the author of the highly successful text, *Personality Theories: Guides to Living.*

1 228119 001 BF

THE GOOD LIFE

Models
For a
Healthy Personality

NICHOLAS S. DICAPRIO

A SPECTRUM BOOK

PRENTICE-HALL, INC., Englewood Cliffs, New Jersey

Library of Congress Cataloging in Publication Data

DiCaprio, Nicholas S
  The good life.

  (A Spectrum Book)
  Bibliography: p.
  1. Personality.   2. Mental hygiene.   I. Title.
BF698.D517   158'.1   76-20591
ISBN 0-13-360396-2
ISBN 0-13-360388-1 pbk.

SUBJECT SPECIALISATION

GLOUCESTERSHIRE
Class 158·1
Copy a
COUNTY LIBRARY

GLOUCESTERSHIRE COUNTY
RESERVE
LIBRARY

*I wish to dedicate this book to Rita, my wife,
and to my children Paul and Laureen.*

© 1976 by Prentice-Hall, Inc., Englewood Cliffs, N.J.

All rights reserved. No part of this
book may be reproduced in any form
or by any means without permission
in writing from the publisher.

A Spectrum Book

10 9 8 7 6 5 4 3 2 1

Printed in the United States of America

Prentice-Hall International, Inc., *London*
Prentice-Hall of Australia Pty. Limited, *Sydney*
Prentice-Hall of Canada, Ltd., *Toronto*
Prentice-Hall of India Private Limited, *New Delhi*
Prentice-Hall of Japan, Inc., *Tokyo*
Prentice-Hall of Southeast Asia Pte. Ltd., *Singapore*

Acknowledgments

I wish to express my deepest gratitude to my many devoted helpers who gave so generously of their time and energies. I am again indebted to Marian Shapiro for her critical help in editing. Her work added significantly to this book. I am also indebted to Jeanne Manson, who worked hard to meet deadlines without complaint. I am especially proud of my students who were so eager to give their assistance. They devoted many long hours of tedious effort. I wish to express my appreciation to Rosemary Sweeney, Jeanne Werwage, and Cindi Smith.

Contents

Preface

This book deals with the ideas of several famous personality scientists concerning two major topics: ideal living and healthy personality growth. We will survey the models of personality used as guides by these specialists in personality treatment. We will consider ideas about the nature and causes of abnormal behavior, in order to apply them to ourselves. The personality scientists spent their professional lives restoring healthy growth and functioning in people suffering from personality disorders. Several of the models deal more directly with the good life and with the highest levels of growth and functioning that are possible for man.

Two objectives will be especially stressed: knowledge of concepts and application of principles to problems of daily living. Essentially, the book deals with the art of living from the perspective and experience of outstanding personality specialists. It presents their insights into the structure, dynamics, and growth of personality.

Most of the chapters follow the same format. A brief introduction and overview of the model sets the stage. This is followed by a consideration of the basic concepts and principles that make up the model. A brief consideration of the meaning of abnormality, according to the ideas of the model, is also presented. Finally, concepts and principles which pertain to the good life and the ideal personality are summarized.

We have chosen several models rather than covering a single model extensively, because human nature takes so many different forms that no single model appears to be sufficient to encompass all people. A person who suffers from a profound sense of inferiority is surely worlds apart from one who has everything except a sense of purpose and meaning to his life. Could the same model apply to a victim of neurosis and to someone who is essentially normal, but who wants a better life for himself?

Actually, we all have several different models of people within ourselves—the normal and abnormal child, adult behavior, appropriate masculine and feminine behavior—models we bring to the various situations and people we encounter. We may not even be aware of their existence, but our own models have a profound influence on our total behavior. However, our own models are usually crude and quite limited. Some elements are given more value than they deserve. The model may contain ideas that are too general to judge and evaluate behavior adequately. We may have too few concepts to deal with the wide differences among people. For example, we may evaluate ourselves and others solely on the basis of a single attribute or quality such as wealth, beauty, wit, or charm. Our models of personality can be expanded and refined by studying those proposed by the experts in personality science.

Most of the models we will consider have one or more distinctive themes concerning the structure, dynamics, and development of personality. Knowing these should give the reader some important "conceptual" tools, as well as refining and sharpening the ones he already possesses. We can learn something from each of the models of the good life and the ideal personality. Furthermore, each model fits some types of people, or perhaps, certain types of problems, better than others. You should "see yourself" in one or more of the models. Each model focuses on a distinctive problem such as striving to overcome inferiority, producing a sense of security, overcoming loneliness, being appreciated by others, reducing tensions and conflict, making good things happen.

These human concerns are like the memorable themes of outstanding classics because they are perennial human aspirations.

One important purpose of the models is to help us understand ourselves and other people. With a knowledge of the models, we are in a better position to look for certain things that we might not otherwise consider. For example, studying the models of personality can help us to identify our underlying assumptions about people: assumptions like everyone is basically selfish; everyone wants to be better than others; everyone wants affection; everyone is capable of real love. Such assumptions may hinder our ability to get to know other people, and for that matter, to know ourselves. We are all psychologists of sorts because we have accumulated knowledge about principles of behavior. But this knowledge may be incorrect or inadequate. We can increase the precision and scope of our knowledge of ourselves and of others through the study of models of personality.

Introduction
To Personality Models

1

If we examine the history of civilization, it becomes quite apparent that man has continually sought to understand himself and his world. The cycles of the seasons, the destructive power of wind and rain, the mysteries of growth and decay, and the vast changes that occur in himself—all these and more have tantalized thoughtful men to seek explanations. Given the ability to perceive, to imagine, to reason, to solve problems, and to anticipate probable future events, man was naturally motivated to try to make some sense of his world and himself. With man's built-in capabilities, it is unthinkable that they would not be used, at first, to unravel nature's secrets, and later to harness those secrets for the betterment of mankind. Furthermore, man is a doer and an inventor; he manipulates and constructs things. The history of man is marked by the development of science and technology. Testimony to man's inventiveness is all about us; all one need do is to look at one's immediate circumstances for ample evidence of man's conquest of nature.

On an individual level, we seek to understand our world and ourselves. For most of us, people are the major source of interest. We are born into a social situation in which other people have tremendous influence. We must learn to understand them, to get along with them, to make adjustments to changes in them and in ourselves. The child attempts to conceptualize his roles in relation to his parents, or to an older brother or sister. These varied relationships must be understood if one is to fit in and get along. But such learning is not supported by systematic teaching. Rather, it is haphazard and often misguided by inconsistencies, injustices, and contradictions. While we spend many years in formal education, some of our most important learning must be acquired without properly trained teachers. Often we are left with the task of teaching ourselves.

We are endowed with intelligence, and we attempt to conceptualize and understand things. We are capable of forming mental representations of things, people, and events. I can look at something and form an image of it. The image may be preserved and later recalled. Man has a phenomenal ability to form concepts which can encompass many different situations, objects, or qualities. We have thousands of words that are used to label our concepts. This amazing ability to represent the things in our world mentally gives man a great potential for knowledge. Thinking and problem solving can occur with the use of mental representations. I can, for example, mentally rearrange the furniture in a room, and can picture whether one arrangement is more suitable than another.

One of our most important concerns is understanding human behavior, our own and others'. Just as we can form mental representations of external events, we can use this capability in understanding experience and behavior. We observe behavior, and we label it. We have terms for various classes and qualities of behavior. We attempt to obtain a picture, or conceptual model, of a person. You might think of the ways you would describe a friend, a teacher, your family doctor, your older sister. We all have our own models of different people. A model of personality is an ordered system of concepts and principles that depict personality make-up and functioning. These concepts and principles are formed through our experiences and personal reflections; but our models are crude, and many of us overgeneralize and overvalue certain qualities, or are limited in our perspective. One of the aims of this book is to examine models that were deliberately formed to describe and explain human behavior. We will be considering the models of personality proposed by well-known psychologists and psychiatrists. By studying the models which experts in the field of personality science have formulated, we can increase our own conceptual tools, and can more effectively understand and deal with ourselves and others.

MODELS OF PERSONALITY

We have all had experiences with models: a model airplane, a model of a submarine, and perhaps a model of a house. The model represents something that is usually too complex or too large to study directly. The good model contains the same features as the thing it represents, so that if we studied the model, we could in fact learn about the thing itself. Before a house is constructed it is usually depicted in a rather complex layout by an architect. The architect may be quite specific in detailing not only exact measurements of rooms, closets, and stairways, but also the types of materials to be used. The "specs," as they are called, may trace the plumbing, the wiring, the heating system, and so on. One who knows how to read such drawings can have a rather complete picture of the house, even though he has not seen the actual home. In the same way, an expert musician can look over an unfamiliar composition and acquire a good picture of how difficult it is. Beethoven, although deaf, was able to compose some of the world's most beautiful music. He was capable of translating musical notes into imagined sound. He could look over a score and obtain an impression of the music.

The architect's drawing and the musical score are models that are very functional because they can be used as guides. Even the slightest deviation from this type of model can cause bad results. Not every model is so exact. Some models are useful because they help us conceptualize or think about the thing we wish to understand. Do we have something that approximates a model of man? It would certainly be helpful in our task of getting to know ourselves and others if we had a model that would tell us what to look for and how to interpret our observations. The fact is that we not only have a model, but several models. The purpose of this book is to highlight the outstanding themes of several well-known models of man. These models are called theories of personality; but for our purpose the terms model and theory will be used interchangeably. Without realizing it, we all have our own general model of man, perhaps several specific models: one for a child, one for members of the same sex and opposite sex, one for elderly people. We even have models for specific classes, such as professors, policemen, the clergy, and so forth.

The Limitations of Our Own Models

When you first meet someone, you quickly begin to form an opinion. You notice his appearance and make a judgment about it. If it is someone of the opposite sex, you immediately apply certain standards of acceptability. The investigation may cease before it gets beyond appearance. Our categories are usually too general: The person is either nice looking or not, bright or not, warm or cold. Such broad classes may force many different people into incorrect categories. We may give more weight than we should to beauty, intelligence, or social charm. Finally, our model may have too few categories to encompass many people; thus we may not feel comfortable relating with children, or with elderly people, or with anyone who falls outside of our limited group. Such a limited model causes serious distortions and misevaluations; we look for the wrong things and generally do not acquire a true picture of personality. One of the major tasks of living is to formulate models that are functional and helpful in revealing the components and operating principles of personality.

Why So Many Models?

If we knew enough about man, it would seem that there should be only one all-encompassing model. But such a possibility is still quite remote. Furthermore, one might question whether a single model could depict such a diversity of types of people. Surely the life style of the airline pilot is radically different from the simple life of a sickly old woman in a nursing home. The nuclear physicist has a very different life style than his young wife who is caring for three active children and keeping house. Compare the child with the mature adult; the neurotic with the highly productive individual; a poor, uneducated person with a wealthy university student. A variety of models is needed to guide us in knowing these various life styles.

One Expert's View

A personality model is one expert's view of the components and operating principles in personality. Most of the models which we will discuss were formulated by personality therapists who devoted their professional lives to attempting to deal with personal problems and to helping people who were having difficulty with living. Their models were functional because they used them as guides. Perhaps we can learn something from them that we can apply to ourselves and others.

Suppose you were planning a trip to a city to which you had never been. If you knew someone in that city, you might ask him to point out places of interest. You are depending upon your friend's experience and good judgment. Being a resident of the city, he should know more about it than you do, and herein lie his personal biases. If he is a teacher, he may believe that the educational institutions are major sources of attraction. On the other hand, if your friend were a naturalist he might point out the park system and places of natural beauty. You might want to see everything, but that is not usually possible; furthermore, not everything is equally worth seeing. Here you can perceive a major problem with personality models: Because human personality is so complex and because there are such wide differences among people, it is possible to stress different aspects. Should we look to an individual's past, because one is, after all, the product of his previous experience? Should we look to the future that a person is working toward? Everyone has some goals that he is trying to attain. Perhaps we should attempt to identify one's important needs and motives because motivation is the driving force behind behavior. What about a person's abilities? Surely they make a difference in total adjustment to living.

Certain models are more useful as guides with certain people. Some of the models explain abnormal aspects of personality. Other models focus more directly on aspects of healthy personality and optimum functioning; thus, such models may be helpful in our own struggle to function well. Yet despite the differences, we can learn something of value from each of the models presented in this book. Each highlights one or more facets of human nature better than the others.

Primary and Secondary Components of Identity

We might propose that each person has an identity, by which is meant certain key traits or characteristics which are almost always present. If any of these are missing, we would immediately perceive a change. We would say that the person is not "himself." Thus, "John is different; he's not as outgoing as he used to be." Just as we recognize one's physical identity by certain characteristics, we also recognize personal identity by stable characterics. It is clear that some things tell us more about a person than others. Whether Mary likes ice cream, candy, and warm baths (secondary components of identity) does not tell us as much about her as her attitude toward saving money, her approach to a difficult task, or her ability to work under pressure (primary components of identity). These aspects of her nature are much more revealing of her personal identity. We might term them aspects of her self, the inner core of her personality. Although her many likes and dislikes are elements of her personal identity, they can change because they are secondary components. An example of the change in primary components might be Mary as a stingy person versus Mary as being very generous. Thus, one means of determining whether we are dealing with primary or secondary components is to ask whether a feature of the personality could be different without significantly changing the total personality. The primary components of personal identity are the most enduring features, the ones which are most characteristic of the person. One of our famous psychologists, Gordon Allport, estimates that there are usually between five and ten primary components of the core self. Each of these central traits is expressed in many ways, of course, and is triggered by a variety of stimuli and situations. We would have to become acquainted with both aspects of these traits to obtain anything like a complete picture of personality. Furthermore, the traits interact, so the task of getting to know ourselves and others well is by no means an easy one. Our knowledge of people should encompass both the significant situations which set off behavior and the components and operating principles of personality itself.

Specific Problems and Proposed Solutions

Each of the personality models appears to highlight a specific problem area and also to offer a comprehensive solution. Again, these problems and solutions are applicable to all of us to some degree, but they are especially relevant for some people.

For example, Erich Fromm sees the major problem of life as loneliness. He believes that everyone strives for relatedness, which means human attachments. Everyone wants to be loved. Here love takes many forms, including brotherly love, motherly love, and love between man and woman. For Fromm, an abundance of love is the only real solution to the problem of loneliness.

Alfred Adler sees the major problem as a profound sense of inferiority. The growing child is continually made to feel his smallness and weakness. All through life we experience inferiority in our dealings with others. Obviously, some people really are inferior to others. There are others who have many favorable qualities but who nevertheless view themselves as inferior. According to Adler, everyone feels inferior but some people use it as a means of escaping or avoiding responsibility. We are counseled by Adler to cultivate courage in facing our problems. Neurosis is a cowardly way of facing life. One may shrink from meeting his problems; he may become sickly and frail. He excuses himself through his illness. Meeting problems head-on is the only answer. Life is an uphill struggle which requires courage and perseverance. Adler also appreciates the natural tendency to be self-centered, and warns against preoccupation with self. He advises parents to cultivate in their children a sense of social responsibility. For everyone, warm social interests and sentiments should temper our fierce personal involvements. Thus, Adler's solution to a sense of inferiority is courage and social sentiments.

Carl G. Jung holds that the major problem of life is one-sided development. In attempting to fit into our various social and work settings, we cultivate a public self that is functional for us. But we may neglect other aspects of our total nature, the more personal ones. Jung believes that we should allow all facets of personality an opportunity for full development and expression. We should neither be overly extroverted nor should we neglect our inner life; we should not focus more attention to intellectual pursuits while neglecting our feelings and emotional life; we should not even attempt to gain conscious control over all aspects of our nature but, rather, we should allow the primitive aspects to express themselves. Full differentiation and integration of personality is the ideal for Jung. Any one-sided emphasis is abnormal; it blocks the fullest growth and expression of personality.

HOW CAN WE USE MODELS OF PERSONALITY?

As we have already noted, a model of personality can serve as a guide that tells us what to look for, and it also keeps us from wasting time observing irrelevant things. Adler tells us that everyone we know and meet must deal with a sense of inferiority. Fromm tells us that everyone experiences loneliness, and so on. Such statements tell us something significant about ourselves and others. Each person expresses inferiority or loneliness in an individual manner. (Knowledge of these proposed principles of behavior draws our attention to specific types of behavior.) A model of personality tells us what to expect. The big difference between a naive observer and one with a guiding model is that the model helps in directing observation. Models of personality provide the user with concepts and principles which describe and explain individual behavior.

Description

The first step in knowing a thing is to describe it. We have terms that describe physical appearance: tall, short, slender, stoop-shouldered, gaunt, haggard-looking, and many more. We have a variety of terms to describe skin, features, facial expression, manner of carrying oneself, body size, and all other physical features. A good model of personality provides the user with terms to describe features of personality. The simplest form of description identifies the parts and gives names to them. Consider one important aspect of personality: feelings and emotions. We have several hundred different words and phrases to name all the varied emotional experiences that are characteristic of humans. Here are just a few: awe, wonder, adulation, joy, love, adoration, hatred, anger, disgust, revulsion, and so on. We also have many words for motivation (impulse, wish, urge, drive), another important aspect of personality. There are different senses, and each has descriptive terms which identify the various sensory experiences: sour, sweet, bright, loud, smooth.

On a more general level of functioning, we have hundreds of trait and type names, such as generosity, stinginess, punctuality, slovenliness, carelessness, irresponsibility, cautiousness, revengefulness, and so on. One psychologist and his students went through the unabridged dictionary and found more than 18,000 terms that describe human behavior.

We may look at Freud's model of personality as a means of obtaining descriptive terms that represent the components of personality. If we wanted some simple terms to use in this description, we might consider Freud's concepts of id, ego, and superego. A little reflection will reveal to us that, although our personality is extremely complex, if we look at it in a general way it can be subdivided into three general aspects: drives, faculties, and conscience. Freud termed the driving forces the id; the psychological faculties of knowing and willing, the ego; and the moral and ethical beliefs, the superego. Both the drives and the conscience attempt to use the ego faculties to carry out their purpose. The id pushes the ego to seek immediate gratification of drive tensions, while the superego works to set the ego against the id urges. Freud was able to clarify many of the things that happen in personality by using these three descriptive terms. He brought out very clearly the pervasive conflicts that rage within the personality and between the person and his environment. These descriptive terms can help us to make a lot of things clear that might otherwise be vague and confusing. We may seek to learn about personality by identifying the operations and interactions of the id, ego, and superego.

Explanation

Probably the most important function of a personality model is its explanatory capability. This aspect of a model will be illustrated by Maslow's motivational scheme; but we will first discuss the nature of explanation in general, and the types of explanations that are relevant to various types of individual behavior—hereditary, environmental, organic, and personality. The models of personality focus most directly on environmental and personality factors.

If I walk into my room and find one of the dresser drawers on the floor with all the contents strewn about, my immediate reaction is disbelief and anger; but after calming down a bit I feel a strong need to know who did it and why. In other words, I am seeking an explanation of what I am observing. I am looking for the cause, and this is precisely what explanation means. To explain means to identify causes.

Two people who are very much in love are usually quite sensitive to each other's behavior, and any discrepancy is usually taken quite seriously. Does he or she really care: "Sometimes I am thoroughly convinced, but at other times I am not sure." Each party demands an explanation of inconsistent moods and behavior. We wish to understand what is going on. Whereas the first step in acquiring knowledge is description, we are not satisfied until we know the reasons why, or, in other words, until we have an explanation.

Man has a strong curiosity need which is also supported by two other needs: to explore things and to manipulate objects. A normal person is constantly seeking to understand the things going on around and within himself. A low level of curiosity is an indication of personality disturbance. Our need to explain is so powerful that we feel tension if it is not satisfied. In fact, we even invent explanations when we do not have the true one. If a friend unexpectedly drops out of school, I begin to search for the possible reasons. Did he run out of money? Could he have eloped? Did he flunk out? Perhaps he just got fed up with the grind. If our curiosity is sufficiently intense, we begin to note things about our friend: He hasn't been himself lately; or he has mysteriously disappeared for the past several weekends. The evidence we put together may lead us to accept a particular explanation; but, of course, until we have the correct explanation, we are guessing. It should be noted, however, that even guesses may vary in degree to which they are supported. Many of the concepts and principles that we will be considering are based on the experience of experts; but they are still only proposed explanations rather than actual facts.

Our interest is in people. We are attempting to understand why we behave as we do. Our general frame of reference is to discover *the conditions and causes of behavior*, our own and others'. As we have noted, it is precisely in this area that personality models can be of most value to us. We are interested in the things that influence our behavior. These are our heredity, our body, our environment, and our personality.

Heredity. We know that our behavior is influenced by our inheritance. We inherit a certain constitutional make-up which continually influences our behavior. A bad mood may be due to our hormones rather than to any bad thoughts or unpleasant experiences. Certain abilities appear to be largely inherited: Thus we may have inherited the muscular apparatus that makes it possible to be an athlete, or the tonal sensitivity that helps to make us a musician. Even general intelligence has a firm basis in our inheritance. If we are trying to identify the causes of certain behaviors, we cannot exclude inheritance.

Body.   Man is a psychobiological unity: The mind and body affect each other. If you are experiencing an emotional upset, your entire body will respond. The skin chemistry changes; your mouth may become dry; you may develop stomach cramps; and your heart may flutter. Likewise, many major disturbances in the body are also reflected in psychological reactions. Fatigue can cause depression, irritability, anxiety, and many other psychological reactions. A headache or a toothache may put you out of commission, so that the only thing you want is relief. We should always be alert to the possibility of organic factors behind behavior. Some people must deal with chronic conditions—such as indigestion, low energy level, and general nervousness—all the time.

Environment.   In attempting to know ourselves and others, we might look for specific situations and the behavior which typically occurs in them. As I get to know John, I can specify pretty much what he will do in a variety of situations. For example, he may become quite angry if he does not get his way; or he may display pleasure when he is the center of attraction. Our immediate circumstances are continually influencing our behavior. The alarm wakes us in the morning, and we begin the day by responding to a host of external stimuli. The open book on the desk reminds us that the work did not get finished because we fell asleep. Next to the book, the letter from a friend sets us to thinking about an overdue answer. The smell of coffee from the kitchen reminds us that time is passing rapidly. Throughout the long and busy day we are bombarded with significant stimuli and situations. A complex or protracted stimulus might be thought of as a situation: a conversation with a rival, an interchange with a professor, being in the cafeteria, and so forth. Our responses to situations become habitual. We may feel depressed on a rainy day, have a bad day on Fridays, and so on. Each one of us has fairly stable patterns of responses to specific situations, and these can be discovered either by us or by another person.

Some of the early psychologists were quite impressed with this model of studying human behavior because it appears to be objective and open. All that one needs to do is simply observe carefully the situation-behavior relationships. It may take several observations of the behavior and event; but with persistence one can get to know himself and others.

Personality. We can make use of the principle that situations influence and control behavior; but the personality itself plays a significant part in behavior. Our attempt to understand ourselves and others would be incomplete if we relied only on observable situations and observable behavior. We have all had the experience of noting a discrepancy between what usually occurred in a given situation and a particular instance in which the person behaved differently. Mary is usually cheerful in the morning, but sometimes she is not. I greet a friend who is usually quite friendly, but on this occasion he ignores me. We can obviously understand that the present response is not just the outcome of the immediate situation, but that it is affected by preceding conditions. Thus my friend might have been in a state of shock as a result of an unexpected poor grade. He did not respond normally because he wasn't in a normal state of mind at the moment. A particular behavior depends upon the context of the continuous flow of behavior. In a sense, each behavior is unique, and each situation is unique. Because recurring situations tend to be similar, and because behavior tends to become habitual, we can look for and expect to find consistency in ourselves and others.

A certain situation may cause one person to be angry while another is not affected at all. The cause for this lies within the personality. The two people responded differently because their personality make-up differs. We are proposing the notion that personality is a "something." It has continuity and identity. We can sense when you are yourself and when you are not. We have many terms that describe or characterize personality. Examples are:

traits, needs, emotions, perceptions, memories, desires, intentions, and so on. We use many adjectives to characterize personality or aspects of it: not only to describe things but also people—generous, miserly, honest, friendly, distant. Such adjectives depict personality as active. Personality itself is another source of behaviors. A talkative person is driven by his desire to converse, so that he actively seeks out opportunities for expressing this trait. One who has a strong need to make money deliberately puts himself in situations in which he can satisfy his need; and so it is with other dynamic aspects of personality.

Maslow's Need Hierarchy

To illustrate the use of a model as a guide to the understanding of personality, we might consider Maslow's concept of need hierarchy.

Maslow maintains that within personality there are different levels of needs. We might imagine a ladder with various rungs. In order to get to the top, we must step on each of the rungs. Maslow's levels of needs vary in strength, so that certain needs take priority over others. If lower needs are strongly deprived, the higher level needs are not even felt, let alone acted upon. He lists five levels, in order of priority: the physiological needs, the safety needs, love and belonging needs, esteem needs, and self- actualization needs. Maslow tells us to look for the existence of such needs and the manner in which they are gratified.

His model tells us, for instance, that the physiological needs are the most potent and take priority over everything else. If you are extremely hungry, thirsty, cold, or in pain, nothing else matters except immediate relief. You are not concerned about your status, your friendships, the condition of your love life, or whether you are satisfying your most basic talents. Your only concern is to find a way of gratifying the physiological need that is occupying the center of your attention.

Once you have satisfied the physiological needs, and only then, do you begin to feel the need for establishing security, building up reserves, working to make the future more comfortable, and in general establishing order and predictability in your life. These are the safety needs.

If your safety needs are sufficiently gratified, the next major area of focus will be your social needs. You may experience acutely the need to be accepted by the people you consider important; and especially important is the need to be accepted and loved by your own peers—and finally by someone of the opposite sex.

Our esteem needs center about gaining respect from others, and ultimately acquiring self-respect. Being accepted and belonging are conditions which lead to the more complex need of wanting to be identified with particular skills or abilities, and so forth.

Only when we have achieved a fairly comfortable status with our lower needs are we capable of experiencing and acting upon the most personal needs, the self-actualizing needs. These needs promote growth and increased participation in things. We might think, for example, of such things as creating; inventing; composing music; being a good parent; being a productive marital partner; and, in general, doing what we consider most fulfilling and most characteristic of self.

Maslow's model not only tells us what to look for in personality, it also gives us a schema to follow. The model serves to guide us in understanding behavior which might otherwise appear inconsistent. Maslow would accept the pervasive roles of the environment, of inherited dispositions, and of the ever-present organic determinants; but he would weave these factors into his own conception of the levels of needs. Using his model should provide a more integrated approach to the study of the determinants of behavior. We can make observations and also interpret them according to this model of need levels. Thus we should be better off than the individual who does not know the model. Its validity, of course, will depend upon its usefulness, and Maslow certainly found it to be a useful guide in his efforts to understand individual behavior. The model is a general framework which we have to particularize for each individual because the circumstances are quite different for each person. But the general pattern of needs and the general statements about them hold for everyone.

SPECIFIC FOCUS

Each model has its own special area of focus: Some deal more adequately than others with personality growth, while some focus on the dynamics of personality. Still others deal with personality when it becomes abnormal or fails to grow properly; and finally, some of the models focus directly on ideal personality and effective living. We should become acquainted with all of these aspects of personality; thus each of the models we will consider has something to teach us. We can profit from the creative genius and extensive experience of such outstanding personality scientists and therapists as Freud, Jung, Erikson, Horney, Adler, Allport, Maslow, Rogers, Fromm, and Skinner. We may occasionally encounter opposing views concerning the explanations of personality phenomena; but since we are dealing with a complex psychobiological organism when we study man, opposing views may reflect opposite types of people.

As you study the various models, you should look for concept terms such as id, ego, and superego, role, self, need hierarchy, the unconscious, and so on. These terms summarize or stand for behaviors; thus you should be able to specify what behaviors are denoted by the id, the ego, or the superego. Concepts help us to comprehend many different behaviors that have something in common.

You will also want to look for working principles. A principle tells you something about the operation or functioning of the components of personality, or about personality in general. An example of a principle is: All behavior is goal-directed. Another is: Behavior is strengthened when it produces rewards. Often you are given concept terms such as id, ego, and superego, and then the operations of these components are elucidated in the form of principles. In other words, you are told something of the nature of these various dimensions of personality. The models contain many concepts and summarize various principles of behavior. Our own model of man should be increased in scope and flexibility by studying the various models that are presented in this book.

PSYCHOLOGY MODELS: EMOTIONAL AND IRRATIONAL MAN

I

We will begin our survey of the models of personality with depth psychology, which is concerned with the nature and operations of the unconscious portions of the mind. It became quite apparent to personality scientists such as Freud and Jung that there was much more to the mind than our conscious thoughts, feelings, and desires. To them, the mysteries of the mind could only be unraveled by plumbing the deepest recesses, the hidden forces that make people behave in strange ways. While other psychologists were trying to learn about man's rational and conscious mental functions, Freud and Jung found that these facets of the mind were not the most fundamental, and that they were, in fact, greatly influenced by the operations of unconscious forces. Freud came to believe that the unconscious mind was always active, and that we experienced its influence most directly in dreams; but he also believed that its operations exert a pervasive influence over conscious experience and behavior all the time. The unconscious becomes most obviously acute in cases of neurosis—unexplained anxieties, irrational wishes and phobias, haunting ideas, and uncontrollable impulses. But we all experience the operation of the unconscious by slips of speech, lapses of memory, unaccountable losses of important things, and even self-defeating behavior such as saying the wrong thing at the wrong time, doing harm to people we love, and resisting authority inappropriately. However, the unconscious is not all bad; it can be beneficial, for from it can come creative ideas and unexplained spontaneous solutions. Freud believed that one may be either in harmony or in conflict with his unconscious mind. Jung went still further in studying the unconscious by tracing its manifestations in the most obscure forms of human expression—mythology, the symptoms of the insane, primitive art forms, symbolic rituals, and the occult. He wanted to get to the very foundation of the psyche itself, to appreciate the origins of human nature.

The Three-Dimensional Self: Sigmund Freud

2

We begin our study of the models of personality with the most controversial and yet the most influential one, that of Sigmund Freud. Freud (1856-1939) lived in Vienna for about eighty years. He trained in medicine, and then specialized in the so-called mental and nervous disorders. Using himself and his patients as subjects of his psychological studies, Freud began to publish his findings and concepts in his late thirties and continued his amazing output through the rest of his life. Freud shocked his medical colleagues with his ideas, and his ideas continue to cause controversy. He became convinced that disturbances in sex were a regular feature of personality disorders; and in many instances, he found that the disorder could be traced to painful early sexual experience. He also stressed the influence on personality formation of early childhood experiences, and maintained that the personality was largely formed by five or six years of age. Perhaps Freud's greatest contribution was his study of the mysterious unconscious forces; he actually came to believe that we have an unconscious mind with a life of its own which continually affects our behavior. Freud found that the baffling and troublesome behavior of nervous patients was caused by unconscious forces over which the person had no control. Although his psychology was derived from maladjusted sick patients, he gradually found that the difference between normal and abnormal is a matter of degree, and that we are all abnormal in some respects. Given stress of sufficient intensity, these symptoms become more exaggerated, and hence more noticeable. He also emphasized the role of conflict in our lives: He felt that our very nature was made up of opposing tendencies that could not be completely eliminated. Conflicts which threaten to tear personality apart exist both within the individual and between the individual and his environment. Freud saw in all of us powerful irrational forces that would make civilized living impossible unless such forces were brought under strict control and properly channeled. Having to work daily with seriously disordered personalities, Freud saw clearly the place of primitive, selfish drives and personal striving.

Freud was a practicing psychiatrist, and in fact, he founded the famous psychoanalytic school. Patients came to him with serious problems related to daily living; but since concepts and techniques for dealing with them did not exist, Freud worked out his own. Freud based his concepts on his observations of real behavior and arrived at them through his creative genius. We can take the same concepts and apply them to our attempts to understand behavior. It should be kept in mind that Freud used his concepts and principles in a practical way—to change the disordered behavior of his patients. It should be possible for us to apply them to our own efforts to change.

We might examine some of the problems that the patients revealed. A young man visited Freud complaining that he was afraid that his wife would leave him because he was incapable of performing the marital act. Although he found his wife highly appealing physically, and even experienced an intense sexual craving for her, he could not perform adequately. This problem is an example of the contradictory character of the types of problems which Freud had to unravel.

Today many people would go to a psychiatrist only after they have consulted several physicians; and of course, in Freud's day, the picture was still worse. Usually Freud dealt with the severely neurotic. A woman came to Freud in a terrible state of nervousness. The woman was suffering from insomnia and heart palpitations. She began to think repeatedly of dying from a heart attack. Freud examined her, and found nothing wrong with her physical condition. He then began to question her life circumstances. One of her persistent worries was that her husband might be unfaithful. She was afraid that he was losing interest in her because there was another woman. As Freud investigated further, he became convinced that there was no real evidence of her husband's infidelity, and that this was her own distorted view of things. But what was behind her false notion? With further probing, it turned out that it was she who had the problem of unfaithfulness. One of the deliverymen had demonstrated some interest in her, and her imagination began to elaborate the seriousness of his intentions. She began to experience a strong romantic attachment for the young man. Because her ego was weak and poorly coordinated, Freud reasoned, she panicked. Her desire for the young man was so difficult to accept that a process of disguise and distortion went to work to convert her unacceptable wish into her husband's infidelity. The woman could be helped only by bringing everything into clear awareness, so that she could examine her real feelings and perceive the situation correctly. Freud believed that unless we continually strive to keep in touch with reality, our fantasies and wishes will take over the mind.

The unconscious mind easily takes over the personality when the ego is weak. The victim may do many irrational and contradictory things. One person may always engage in behavior that causes him problems—such as quitting a fine job just when things begin to look good. Another person is always getting into accidents, or losing things, or forgetting important engagements, and so on. In some people, the unconscious seems to arrange unfavorable outcomes. In many instances, the person could do a better job even if he had deliberately set out to hurt himself. Yet in some people the unconscious mind seems to be the source of creative ideas and intuitions. We will consider the unconscious further because it was the cornerstone of Freud's psychology; in fact, Freud's psychology could be described as the psychology of the unconscious.

BASIC CONCEPTS & PRINCIPLES
LEVELS OF AWARENESS

Consciousness

We all experience the relentless flow of our stream of consciousness. It keeps us in touch with ourselves and with the outside world. Psychologists have long been concerned with these subjective states. Today, we hear a great deal about altered states of consciousness—of increased awareness, of mind-expanding drugs, of higher states of consciousness, of being "stoned," and "turned on." We can sense that our immediate experience ebbs and flows and depends upon external and internal factors, some of which we can control. But we often are acutely aware of our lack of control when unwelcomed thoughts force themselves on us. Even when we attempt to force them back, we encounter failure. Freud found, for example, that the explanation of behavior, particularly the abnormal behavior of his patients, could not be accounted for by conscious motives or desires. It was this type of experience that led Freud to infer the existence of a dynamic unconscious; and so, rather than studying consciousness, Freud became much more concerned with the unconscious.

The Preconscious

Present attention is usually limited to one particular thing. Psychologists have long accepted the principle that we can only really focus attention on one thing at a time. Attention has both a focus and marginal elements, however; there is constant shifting. The term preconscious stands for ordinary recall. Ideas are preconscious when we are not thinking of them. Both external and internal stimuli will bring them to the surface. Such preconscious memories are distinguished from unconscious material in that they are capable of recall. The point is that some experiences which cannot be retrieved even by the ordinary memory techniques may have harmful effects on both conscious experience and behavior.

The Unconscious

Studying neurotics, it became apparent to Freud that unconscious factors were at work producing the symptoms. An unsettling experience might be so charged with anxiety that the individual could not deal with it consciously. A disturbing situation produces tension that continues until there is some kind of resolution. But, if the ego is weak, it may deal with the experience by repressing it, which means to *exclude* it from awareness. Though unconscious, the repressed material may have the same effects as if it were conscious. I might be unconsciously angry toward a friend and do many of the same things that I would do if the anger were conscious, the only difference is that the anger is not directly experienced. My reactions might be contradictory: I might get irritated with my friend for no apparent reason; my mood may become depressed in his presence, and so on. The anger remains in the unconscious as a constant source of disturbance.

The operation of a disturbing unconscious motive may cause two people in a dating relationship to continue seeing each other, even though there is a great deal of friction between them. Freud might point to the unconscious motivation in both parties to retaliate for the uncertainty of each other's feelings. The desire to injure seems to be the only factor that keeps the relationship going.

Freud makes an extremely important point about the persistence of unconscious motives. Frequently, he found that, instead of "new living" occurring in new situations, what actually takes place is the reawakening of an old conflict or motive. He came to the conclusion that unconscious material is preserved in a dynamic rather than an inactive form.

We have witnessed many cases of killings of close relatives and friends. This puzzling phenomenon may be explained in Freud's concepts. A man purchases a gun for the purpose of protecting his family, which is an acceptable motive to his ego. He does not secure the gun to kill his wife; that would not be an acceptable motive. Yet one night they have a quarrel, and he becomes so furious that he reaches impulsively for the gun and kills his wife. He experiences a great deal of remorse afterward. It is likely that he was harboring a great deal of unconscious hate for his wife, hate which was being held back by ego forces, but which found direct outlet when he became angry. Many of our repressed motives are of an aggressive nature and constantly threaten to break through. Just as one may be injured by environmental circumstances over which there is no control—war, depression, inflation—so one may also be victimized by his unconscious. One cause of this condition is an ego that learns to avoid rather than to face problems.

Bodily, a person may be reacting with strong emotions even though he experiences no conscious hostility. One who is bitter regarding his lot in life, although the feeling remains unconscious, has the same bodily reactions as a person who feels the same emotions consciously. The body takes a terrible beating under these conditions, and a so-called psychosomatic disorder may develop. These disorders have been called stress reactions because the victim appears to be under more tension than he can adapt to. Whether the emotional cause is consciously felt or not makes no difference with respect to organic reactions. These disorders are all the more puzzling when the external situations do not appear to be stressful.

Repression

During the last part of the nineteenth century, the bacterial agents which caused several infectious diseases were discovered. This breakthrough in physical medicine suggested to Freud that there might be an analogous process behind mental and emotional illness. It occurred to him that repression might be the cause which underlies many personality disturbances. A repression is an unconscious motive or conflict which exerts a harmful effect on experience and behavior. The repression is like a poisonous agent whose effects can actually interfere with the most basic psychological processes, such as perception itself. Healthy functioning can only be restored if the repression is uncovered and neutralized.

Here is a typical case in which repression played a significant role. A young woman visited Freud suffering from a paralysis of an arm which interfered with her domestic duties, as well as causing her a great deal of pain. Being trained as a physician, Freud examined her arm, but found nothing wrong. The skin color was fine, all reflexes were normal, and the muscle tone was excellent. What could cause the problem? It would make no sense to assume that she was consciously desiring her illness, so the only other alternative was an unconscious wish to be ill. Freud inquired into her immediate circumstances. It turned out that she was the only child of an invalid, widowed father, and custom dictated that she care for him. She had a suitor who wished to marry her, but she would not give him a definite answer because she could not resolve the conflict in which she found herself. He eventually broke off their relationship, which was a highly painful experience for her, and it was soon afterward that she developed the physical symptoms. Freud interpreted the situation as an instance of repression. The young woman was certainly in a difficult situation because she could not resolve the conflict between duty to her father and her natural desire for marriage. Furthermore, she resented her role as servant to her father, and these feelings were so unacceptable to her that she repressed them. When the conflict was intensified by the breakup of the relationship, it became converted into a physical illness which, though painful, did relieve some of the tension. Had she married the young man and then become afflicted with the paralysis, she would have been a poor wife. Now that she was an invalid herself, she no longer could care for her father. The repression itself created new problems for her—invalidism—and in fact, did not really solve her original ones.

As we have noted, Freud viewed normal and abnormal as a mat-

ter of degree; thus repression is not to be viewed only as a highly
pathological condition, but rather as a common occurrence of
everyday life. A man goes shopping for his wife, and strangely he
meticulously buys everything on the list except her cigarettes.
When he gets home, a big scene occurs because he does not want
to go back to the store. He pleads that it was an honest mistake,
and argues that it would not hurt her to give up cigarettes for the
weekend. Being a non-smoker, he finds smoking obnoxious; and
the hold that it has over his wife and other smokers puzzles him.
She finally storms off to the store for herself. This rather uncomplicated event of everyday life can be interpreted in terms of the
process of repression. How would you account for this behavior?
The husband would probably admit that he really wished that his
wife would stop smoking; but he would hasten to add that he was
not trying to force her to do so, and that he certainly did not deliberately forget her cigarettes. But the event did occur, and it must
have an explanation. Freud observed that this type of forgetting
was different from the ordinary type because it served a purpose.
The perceptual operation of the ego was temporarily interfered
with by the unconscious purpose, causing him not to react to the
written item on the list.

One form of preventing repression is to desensitize painful
experiences rather than simply putting them out of mind, or just
forgetting about them. If one simply attempts to forget painful
past experiences, new situations will inevitably reactivate the old
memories in one form or another. A child who has never really
dealt with his negative emotions toward his father may always be
vulnerable to situations in which an authority must be obeyed. In
such situations, the negative emotion will interfere with intelligent
behavior. Further, the lack of awareness of the disturbing cause
will make the relationships with authority figures still more puzzling and difficult to deal with. The repression acts like an independent agent in the unconscious that is dynamically active in a
variety of situations. The aphorism, "forgive and forget," is effective only if the forgiving really involves a desensitization of the
painful emotion. Therefore, it is advisable, occasionally, to re-
experience in thought or imagination a bad past situation so that it
can be neutralized emotionally. The best time for this cleansing, so
to speak, is during states of well-being and calm. It is possible to

induce such states by learning techniques of relaxation, and then mentally reviewing the painful events which one wishes to neutralize. Some forms of meditation can also be used for the same purpose.

Relationships Between Conscious and Unconscious Mind

It is interesting to contemplate that we have, in a sense, an unconscious mind with many layers, which perhaps, has a life of its own. Suppose you wish to recall a phone number: You are asking your unconscious mind, which stores it, to get it for you. At times, it comes immediately; and at other times, you may get the answer much later, when you are thinking of something else. Frequently, of course, we do not get the memory at all. Even solving a problem involves a searching process. You cannot force the answer to come. We may even sense that the memory and solution are there, but they do not come immediately.

The unconscious mind might be considered as an "intimate friend," one which plays an important part in maintaining the organism. The conscious mind has its jobs to do—keeping in touch with the external world, regulating the satisfaction of needs, resolving conflicts, and so on. The unconscious, too, has its tasks, such as coming up with memories and solutions to problems, regulating the complex organs of the body, and so on. As we have noted, Freud found that opposition could exist between the conscious and unconscious mind: The person might frequently engage in self-defeating behavior, choose the wrong alternative, and experience anxiety and conflict. Such a person might be described as not being on friendly terms with his unconscious. On the other hand, the two can work harmoniously, like intimate friends. Keeping this in mind, one should be friendly toward his unconscious, and let it work for him. One should not be constantly self-critical. If there is a problem, allow the unconscious time to come up with the solution. Many creative people have reported that they can rely on the unconscious for answers.

As mentioned previously, ideas may break into consciousness which cause tension and disturbance. We might unwillingly experience thoughts of death, of illness, of aging, of the futility of living, and so on. These thoughts exist in the fringe areas of consciousness for all of us. How can we keep them from obtruding into the center of our consciousness? One point is clear: A busy and active consciousness is not as troubled by these disturbances as one which is morbid and inward. Unwelcome intrusions from the preconscious fringe, and especially from the deeper layers of the unconscious, are blocked by an active imagination, productive thinking, having many things to do, and working toward clearly defined goals.

We may use the analogy of a well-run home. If everyone is contributing and things are kept in order—bills paid, doors and windows locked, children properly cared for—then danger is averted. But if these things are not done, alien forces take over: The home is burglarized, the children get sick, and smooth functioning ceases to occur. Unwelcome thoughts of inferiority, futility, and death are the aliens we wish to keep out of our mental household, and the way to do so is to make consciousness dynamic and active.

Make-Up Of Personality

If we examine our own experience through the Freudian model, we might arrive at the same discovery that Freud made concerning personality. We might find that we have three selves: a lower self, a controlling self, and a higher self. Furthermore, we would probably find that these selves have different objectives and are in conflict with each other. The lower self consists of strong drives that make themselves felt insistently in consciousness; at times, these drives produce so much tension that nothing else matters except getting relief. You might recall an instance of extreme hunger, or thirst, or severe pain. During such times, moral considerations, and even reality itself, may be completely disregarded.

Another self is the ego, which is the controlling self, the controlling agent within the personality. Further, it is the controlling agent in the center of consciousness. You experience the controlling self as a problem-solver in touch with the external world. It comes between one's instinctual drives and the demands of the external world, and its purpose is to satisfy the requirements of the person without incurring injury.

The third self is the higher self, or the better self, which Freud terms the superego. We experience this self as conscience and as "oughts" and "shoulds." It is the self which we would like to become. For example, we experience our higher self when we help someone in need. We also feel good about ourselves and experience pride.

Freud viewed personality as being made up of warring factions. He treated these three components as if they were independent sub-personalities competing relentlessly for the existing psychic energy. Each of the three selves represents enduring tendencies within personality. In a sense, each self opposes the aims of the other selves. Thus, inherent in the very make-up of personality are the ingredients for conflict, both internal and external. The id, or the lower self, is roughly the biological self. It is the primary personality, and always remains the most personal and organic in that its demands cannot be done away with. It becomes active when the needs of the body reach a certain intensity. The ego or the controlling self is roughly equivalent to the psycho-social self. It is the administering agent in control of the higher psychological functions. The superego, or the higher self, is the moral-ideal self. It encompasses two important aspects of personality: a sense of conscience, and the ego ideal, which is the perfected self. The id, then, consists of strong urges which press for direct outlet. The ego attempts to find acceptable outlets for, and maintains control of, the id. The superego pressures the ego to follow moral standards and ideals and it opposes direct expression of the id. Freud views the origin of neurosis to be, in part, caused by the rivalry of the competing selves.

Conflicts Between the Three Selves

A little self-observation should quickly convince you of the divisions within your personality. How often do you do things which afford immediate relief of tension, but which create problems in the future? How often have you taken shortcuts and the easiest way out of the present situation, but at the expense of more pain later? A man reported that he had to be constantly on guard against his weaknesses and his "irresponsible" self (his lower self). He worked out ways of making sure that he did not drink too much when he was out with his associates. When he put something aside, he made a note of it, so that he would not forget the task, particularly if it were a distasteful one. Finding that he frequently misplaced things, he made a point of putting important things only in specific places, so that when he searched for them he could run through the various storing places.

We might enumerate hundreds of instances which involve conflict between an apparently lower self and a higher self, with the controlling self in the middle, trying to harmonize conflicting goals. We must all learn to manage ourselves in order to keep out of trouble and to meet our needs. In early life, much of this is done by others; but as the superego develops and as the ego increases in strength the control is within the person. But pleasure-seeking in all its various forms can trick us into following our impulses and get us into difficulty.

The ego is vulnerable to many hurts. It develops protective strategies which have been termed defense mechanisms. We may think of these defense strategies as signs of weakness, yet they can be extremely important in meeting the requirements of living. If we feel chilly, we immediately take action to change the situation. We may put on a sweater, turn up the thermostat, close the window, and so on. But what about painful experiences which cannot be avoided, and which may not be our fault? Surely there must be ways of protecting against these. We use an umbrella in the rain, a coat in winter, a hat to protect against the sun. Why not defense mechanisms to protect against needless disappointment, grief, sadness, and a sense of inferiority? Faced with such problems, we can use reason to solve them and to protect ourselves when no solution is possible.

Conflict Between Reality and Pleasure

Freud was very much impressed with the ever-present conflict between the requirements of reality and the pursuit of pleasure. He stressed tension reduction as the major source of pleasure motivation; but he came to appreciate the role of positive tension and pleasurable stimulation as sources of pleasure. The arousal of a motive is experienced as tension, and the tension itself serves as a drive for relief. We desire relief as quickly and as directly as possible. Reality, on the other hand, is accepted only because of necessity. One of our most typical conflicts is the opposition between the desire for pleasure and the requirements of reality. The pleasure may be so tempting that it overrides realistic considerations.

One of the major tasks of the ego is impulse control and keeping the level of excitation down. In the process of finding an adequate outlet for tensions, the ego must endure the tension. Contrast the behavior of a two-year-old with a mature adult: The two-year-old expresses impulses directly and immediately. We do not hold the child accountable for his impulses, even when they cause damage. The child is judged with the view that his ego has not taken over the management of his personality. The normal adult is expected to tolerate frustration until he finds some type of outlet. Even when the direct outlet is not available, impulsive outbursts are not permitted. The tension must be endured while he seeks a substitute outlet.

As the child grows older, more and more is expected of him. He is held accountable for impulse control. For instance, if he displays anger toward his parents or teachers, he may be punished. When something is not available, the older child is expected to accept reality and not cry. The id always presses for immediate gratification; but the ego must face reality and the consequences of unlimited and impulsive expression. Pleasure-seeking, which includes tension reduction, is subject to many conditions and restrictions in the mature person.

The Controlling Self, Anxiety, and Defense Mechanisms

The major task of the controlling self is to administer the personality. Everything comes to a head in the controlling self. Instinctual drives are felt in the controlling self as tension; the demands and pressures of the external world often produce anxiety (worry and fear) in the controlling self; conscience causes guilt and feelings of unworthiness in the ego; failure to live up to expectations of the better self causes guilt and self-disapproval. The ego is also the focus of conflicting tendencies: the ever-present desire for pleasure exerted by the lower self and the requirement to keep in contact with reality. A moral requirement is also usually present: One therefore finds difficulty harmonizing pleasure with the demands of reality, and, at the same time, following a moral code which may be even more restrictive than reality itself.

Anxiety. When the ego is in danger of too much tension from the various sources noted above, it experiences anxiety. Anxiety may be considered as psychic pain—worry, nervousness, dread, discomfort. Because it is a painful state, anxiety motivates us to do something to get rid of it. Often, the best way is to take direct action to change the instigating condition—by satisfying a need, by meeting some requirement of the external world, or by giving in to the expectation of conscience. Frequently, a direct response is not possible, for many reasons—lack of knowledge, skill, courage, energy, appropriate object, and so forth—and anxiety builds up. As Freud observed, an interesting thing happens: Rather than dealing with the problem, the ego may resort to defense mechanisms.

Defense Mechanisms. These mechanisms, which are not innate but learned, work directly on reducing the anxiety and protecting the ego. They might be thought of as pain killers because they deal directly only with the felt tension rather than with the underlying problem. They give temporary relief. Learning to reduce tension by means of defense mechanisms occurs rapidly, because relief follows immediately and is quite complete for the time being. One more point before we consider some of the major mechanisms: Defense mechanisms tie up useful energy and limit what is available for productive activity. An outstanding characteristic of a disordered personality is the inability to use psychological abilities fully.

1. *Rationalization.* Rationalization does not mean acting rationally, but rather using rationality or reason to make your

behavior appear rational to yourself and others. This mechanism might be described as making excuses, as self-justification, as camouflaging motives, or as self-deception.

When a task is especially difficult, the tension which is experienced may goad the person to put it off. Simply turning away from a task is not acceptable in itself for many people, so they find an excuse, a good reason to postpone the task. Being tired, not having enough time to get very far, having some other more pressing things to do, and so on are typical rationalizations. The more clever the individual is, the more sophisticated are the rationalizations he can create for himself. The famous German poet, Goethe, pointed out that: "Man would have lived better if thou hadst not given him that gleam of heavenly life which he called reason; which he uses only to be more animal than any animal."

Of course, the term paper does not get written, or the bills do not get paid, but only those tensions that are most intense are relieved. We make up excuses for everything imaginable: for poor grades, for failure of all sorts, for violating the law, and even for serious misconduct. The self is protected, but the problems are still unmet.

2. *Projection.* What is inside of us is often perceived as being external. We often see our own faults in others, and, at the same time, we do not perceive them in ourselves. The image on the screen comes from the projector. In the same way, a person with a fault may see it in others who actually do not possess this fault. Think, for example, of such terms as blaming others and fault-finding. You are angry and accuse your friend of being irritable: You may be projecting your own inner turmoil. The flirtatious female accuses all men of having only one thing in mind: She may be revealing her own unconscious need. Jealousy is often an instance of projection: The person has temptations of infidelity; he sees his own struggle in the other person, and accuses his partner of being unfaithful. Knowledge of self requires that we perceive our own faults; but the mechanism of projection interferes with this objective because it allows us to ascribe our faults to others. Incidentally, the mechanism of projection also impairs our knowledge of others because we see things that are not there. The projection, so to speak, gets in the way and causes us to distort our perception of ourselves. Then, too, if we see the fault in the other,

we might permit ourself to retaliate against him. Scapegoating, which means blaming someone (and even an entire group) for one's problems, is a form of projection. Self-knowledge and projection cannot exist together.

3. *Reversal of Motives.* Freud was especially fond of uncovering disguises and pointing them out. One disguise which is especially intriguing is the reversal of motives. Most of us have probably experienced the uncertainty of our feelings toward a friend. Do we really like or dislike him? It appears that opposites in the psyche are often closer than the intermediate states, for sometimes a complete reversal takes place rather suddenly. Two ardent lovers may suddenly engage in a vicious argument and rage at each other, even though they were getting along quite well up to that point. Very often, the basis of a motivational reversal is an unacceptable emotion or motive which is unconscious. The boss who is a great advocate of order and precision at work may live chaotically at home. One who vehemently criticizes pornography may convince himself that he should become acquainted with the problem and so undertake to accumulate a good sized collection. The person who is "against" somebody or something is often strongly fighting his own forbidden desires. Sometimes, we are overly kind to those we dislike, perhaps to protect against the outpouring of our real feelings. Such reversals because they are disguises, are always vulnerable to discovery: Thus the person who is the victim of reversals must be constantly on guard against his real impulses. This situation is not satisfactory for positive ego functioning.

4. *Displacement.* A man working all day under very frustrating conditions comes home with a great deal of pent-up tension. His wife meets him at the door with a list of complaints, which only creates more frustration and more tension. Angrily, he rushes to his room, throws some clothes into a suitcase, and bolts out the door. His wife is terribly upset and confused, and so is he. After a few hours of "cooling off" in a hotel room, he begins to experience guilt and worry about what he did and about how he will spend the next few days. Here we have an example of what Freud called displacement. Displacement refers to a substitute outlet for emotional tension associated with a particular need. The man was

angry with his boss, but was unable to discharge the emotional tension, so it stayed with him until he got angry with his wife and then he took direct action. In a real sense, his wife became the substitute object for the tension that was caused by his boss. Since learning is often instigated by the necessity of finding harmless displacements, we must find better and better ways of satisfying our most personal impulses, because a substitute usually leaves a residue of frustration.

Certainly the displacement of anger used by the harrassed husband only created further tensions. Perhaps his wife should have waited until he had recovered his composure before confronting him with the day's problems. Learning how to relax both body and mind is a good way to get rid of some of the inevitable free-floating tension. Vigorous exercise is also good, as is a hot shower or bath. Some people find blessed relief from drinking or drugs, but there are some other potential dangers with these methods. The tension relief may be so pleasant that the person concentrates on the enhanced psychic state more than he does on solving his problems. In any case, displacements vary in their adequacy to serve the end of healthy functioning.

5. *Sublimation.* We must find outlets for impulses that are not acceptable in their direct form. The mature person is one who denies neither his impulses nor the social restrictions on those impulses, but who finds good sublimations, and thereby reduces the conflicts in his life. Suppose a young wife cannot have children of her own. She might respond with a number of possible abnormal behaviors: She may treat a pet dog like a child, spend a lot of money on stuffed animals, or on the other hand, she might volunteer to care for orphan children. She can give them all the love she would give her own, and, at the same time, be doing highly commendable work.

A person is fortunate if he can discover sublimations for his frustrated drives or ambitions. Our society does provide many outlets for those who are perceptive enough to take advantage of them. Consider the case of the critic: Many literary critics are really frustrated authors; many music critics would have preferred to be performers. We certainly can work off some of our tension through sublimation. It is unwise and potentially dangerous to express our needs in their primitive form, but through sublimations we find a more refined outlet.

IDEAL PERSONALITY AND LIVING

The Normal Ego

Freud held that the ego should be strong and uninhibited. The ego should live harmoniously with the superego; in fact, the opposition between them should be so minimal that they eventually become one and the same. The controlling self and the ideal self should merge. If one tempers his conscience and brings ideals into line with real potential, then the superego will not be oppressive. The ego, too, must increase its strength and develop its potentialities fully. It should attain easy gratification of impulses, and find suitable sublimations for the forbidden ones. In relation to the id, the ego should channel impulses so that it does not become overwhelmed by them. Denial and repression are cowardly ways of dealing with impulses. Rationality should be used not as much for defense and ego protection as for meeting the needs of the organism. In relation to all the components of personality and the external world, the ego should be the master. This means giving a hearing to all factions, compromising at times, being assertive at other times, and being willing to suffer frustration, pain, disappointment, and failure. Freud believed that ultimately we must face reality squarely and be willing to take sorrow and frustration, because these potential difficulties are part of living as self-conscious and future-oriented beings.

Attributes of Maturity

Freud was once asked what a mature person was like. After some thought, he answered that a mature person should be capable of working productively and of loving. This formula for the ideal personality and the good life may seem too simple to be valid. Both attributes, however, require many favorable traits and achievements.

In order to work productively, one must be able to tolerate frustration and tension, because mistakes will inevitably occur. One should be capable of resisting distraction and of persevering in spite of obstacles. One must be able to get to places promptly and to apply oneself fully. Work involves concentration, effort, planning, training, and much more.

An intimate and loving relationship also requires many favorable traits such as respect for another, the ability to see the world from the standpoint of other people, the ability to give up personal desires for the sake of a loved one, and the ability to sacrifice and give of oneself. Freud placed special significance on mutually satisfying sexual activities in marriage, not only because of the basic physiological drive, but also because the most distinctively human attributes are required for success in this most important aspect of married life. For Freud, general maturity was equal to heterosexual maturity; but again one should bear in mind that many requirements must be met to attain satisfactory sexual union. A child is certainly not capable of heterosexual love in any meaningful sense. If the earlier traits are not adequately developed— trust, courage, tenacity, self-love—and/or if there are unusual difficulties in adolescence, several abnormal traits may develop: sentimental love and the idealization of marriage, indiscriminate hate and bitterness, compulsive work or the inability to work for a sustained period. Fixation during adolescence results in a juvenile personality, characterized by extreme idealism, disturbed social relationships, changeability of goals and values, and disturbance in personal identity. It is interesting to note that all of these abnormalities are related to work and love.

Ego Development and Fixation

The development of the ego is a lengthy process, involving a vast amount of learning. We learn concepts, attitudes, skills, sensory discriminations, things to avoid, and even irrational behaviors and defenses. We have many teachers, but not all know how to teach. We learn a great deal through observing and imitating. We also learn through rewards and punishment. Emotional responses are often learned through a special type of learning called conditioning, which consists of transferring an intense response caused by an emotional situation to a neutral stimulus which was present. For example, an unpleasant experience with a math teacher may transfer to mathematics in general and may create a permanent learning block. Freud accepted these various forms of learning; but he also introduced a special process which is behind much learning—fixation. Fixation refers to the cessation of growth, or stunting, which may occur in the development of a particular need or trait. Fixation is not to be understood simply as a lack or deficiency, but rather as an active force in the personality. Lack of adequate mothering in infancy may produce a fixation of the need for mothering, with the result that the person may continually look for comfort and support from others. The immature person has many fixations, while the mature person has relatively few. Again, for Freud, normality and abnormality is a matter of degree.

Freud proposes the interesting notion that traits of personality result from the manner in which certain important needs are gratified: If a need is frustrated too much or indulged too much, then there is a fixation of that need. The needs emerge as certain body organs become important in the life of the growing child. The earliest needs center about mouth activities—feeding, swallowing, erupting teeth, spitting out, and so forth. Freud believed that certain important traits have their origin in this period. The traits have to do with receiving and taking things, and also include such basic traits as optimism-pessimism, cynicism-gullibility, envy, and sarcasm. For example, a person who continually grumbles about his lot in life may be a victim of oral fixation as a result of frustration in feeding experiences. The next organ of the body which becomes important is the anus. This is the period of cleanliness training, and again, Freud relates certain important traits to this period, including neatness, promptness, compliance, and orderliness. Fixation at this stage leads to exaggerated needs and abnormal traits and behaviors. Everyone knows a person who is orderly, compulsive and stubborn; Freud would relate these traits to early frustration in toilet training. The next organs to cause concern and become the focus of needs are the genitals. Self-stimulation and curiosity can produce pleasure and/or punishment. Fixations during this period produce traits which lead to abnormal behaviors relating to self-feelings, social relationships, and difficulty with authority. One result of fixation on this level is too much self-love or conceit.

These three stages take place during the first six years. Freud felt that between six and twelve the child goes through a consolidation period in which many skills and ideas are learned, but that nothing basically different takes place with respect to new needs and traits. The final period of development of the personality begins with adolescence, when the sexual needs become more active. Interest in the other sex develops and becomes more focused. Any fixations will hamper both social and sexual maturity. Freud believed that, because the process of development is so protracted in man and the hazards are so great, no one makes the journey to adulthood without some fixations.

The adult personality is highly complex. We might appreciate this complexity by thinking of a complicated model airplane. It may have several hundred pieces that are glued together. If any are missing, the final product will be less than complete, or misshapen. If it happens that some of the pieces are not the proper size, this too will cause distortion. Freud held that each stage of development contributes some essential ingredients to the total personality and the fully developed ego. Certainly optimism is required to overcome the disappointments of life; tenacity helps us to stay with our problems until we find solutions; courage and self-confidence are also attributes that help us to overcome obstacles. The latest acquisitions are the ability to work productively and to love; and these add new dimensions to the developing personality. Freud has delineated the various traits that are required for maturity and adult living. We can examine our behavior in various situations with these traits in mind.

SELFHOOD

The concept of selfhood is not often used in connection with Freud's model of personality, but it is certainly applicable to his ideas on fulfillment and maturity. The id, ego, and superego represent the conflicting factions in personality. When the ego becomes the true ruling force in personality, when the superego has been made conscious and has been changed to meet the demands of the ego, when the impulses of the id are properly experienced and sublimated, and when repressions are finally eliminated, then the person has attained selfhood. He has become a self-fulfilled, socialized, and contributing member of his community. The conflicts which raged so violently during the maturing process are considerably diminished. The person is integrated and at peace with himself; and at the same time, he lives harmoniously in his environment. In other words, he has reduced the internal and external conflicts to the point where he can use all his abilities fully, as well as develop his potentialities. Agreeing with Jung, Freud found that in this state, the person is not troubled by the artificial standards and expectations of the culture; rather, he determines his own destiny. If happiness is to be attained, it can only occur when selfhood is achieved. The ego becomes the master of the two intrapsychic tyrants—the id and the superego—which constantly plague it. The ego is also freed to deal with external forces and frustrations as it goes about the task of administering the personality.

Archetypes and the Collective Unconscious: Carl Gustav Jung

3

The ideas of the Swiss psychiatrist, Carl Gustav Jung (1875-1961) are beginning to receive increasing attention among personality scientists and intellectuals. In attempting to understand and treat the human psyche, Jung followed unorthodox paths of investigation. He even took several sojourns to live with and study the life style of primitive tribesmen. Believing that the current image of man as a fully conscious and rational being is incomplete, Jung sought to discover man's true nature by observing his origins as well as his more fundamental expressions. Everything man does and produces can reveal something of his nature; thus Jung was led to study primitive rituals, ceremonial practices, mythology, symbology, alchemy, the occult, astrology, ESP, UFO's and even mediums. He believed that all these are legitimate expressions of the human psyche and, therefore, that they must reveal the real nature of man. Jung believed that consciousness and rationality are late evolutionary processes in man. He felt that we do not lose the primitive aspect of our nature, however; and he warned that unless we discover what that primitive aspect is and find adequate expression of its requirements, we will continue to experience the numerous ills of our times. Jung held that the major upheavals of this century were not caused by a few perverted minds, but were the outcome of human requirements that were being denied and frustrated. Jung was both pessimistic and optimistic for the future: His pessimism stems from the terrible record of man's inhumanity to man, which continues to show no abatement; his optimism derives from the great potential that man has demonstrated both collectively and individually. We already possess vast knowledge and technology, which could foster growth and fulfillment. We are facing a highly critical period because the destructive forces appear to outweigh the constructive. Jung was convinced that if we can survive a few more years, the tide will change.

Jung, like all the outstanding personality scientists, well appreciated the powerful forces of society. What society stresses does not necessarily promote the individuated personality, which was Jung's ideal for man. Jung believed that if one gives himself fully to the pursuit of society's values, the cost is usually a personality and life that is one-sided and incomplete. The person who sacrifices the most important things in life for the sake of a career may realize when it's too late that he paid a supreme price for his success. Jung stressed the fullness of growth and the expression of all aspects of personality. Any one-sided emphasis, he felt, would hinder the individuation process, resulting in symptoms of maladjustment.

Jung, like Freud, found that consciousness was not by any means the whole of personality. However, Jung went even further than Freud in his investigations of the nature of the unconscious mind in the study of the collective unconscious. He had the knack of getting into the most remote topics, those which other scientists considered unworthy of scientific attention; but he found them to be rich sources of knowledge about the hidden recesses of personality, the very foundation of the human psyche.

Jung had wide clinical experience, and he wrote extensively. His ideas have not yet reached their fullest recognition; the true worth of his work has yet to be determined.

BASIC CONCEPTS AND PRINCIPLES

Like Freud, Jung wanted to learn about personality make-up and dynamics from his patients; their treatment sessions were essential learning experiences for him. From his observations, Jung formulated concepts and principles to describe and explain the many puzzling things he observed. His concept terms, as mysterious and abstract as they seem, must be understood as representing real behaviors. For example, he discovered in men certain feminine traits which can produce highly disturbing symptoms. He called these traits anima traits, which are defined by specific behaviors. A man who has underdeveloped anima traits will behave differently from one who has normal anima traits. The man who tries to play a supermasculine role may at times display childish and stubborn behaviors. Jung would ascribe these behaviors to the undeveloped feminine traits in the man.

Jung viewed personality as highly complex. If you ask a person to tell you about himself, what he usually describes is the social personality. The person might identify himself with a particular vocation or profession such as accountant, lawyer, teacher, or student. He may reveal some of his likes and dislikes. He may go on to tell about some of his attitudes and values. He may even say something about his faults; but here we begin to see some hesitation and confusion. Those who know that person might disagree with his account of his shortcomings and weaknesses. The person might be aware, to some degree at least, of his moods—of those times when he is "not himself." But again, this aspect of his personality is not as clear to him as is the more social side of his nature. Almost certainly an objective observer would see much more than the person himself would see. It was this type of observation that led Jung to view personality as made up of many systems, and to recognize that some of these systems were not expressed fully or even acknowledged by the ego. A person might be primarily an actor, playing out a social role. He might block other conflicting aspects of his personality from consciousness because they were considered unacceptable. Jung found that one of the major tasks of personality therapy was to help his patients discover what he called the "members of the household of personality." Step by step, the person comes to learn and experience all the components and aspects of his personality. This process is often quite painful because the very things that must be experienced are blocked from consciousness. They are kept out because the person does not want to know them.

Some of the Objectives
of a Jungian Analysis

Jung believed that, in the process of adapting to the demands of our culture, we may lose our wholeness or individuality. One of the most important tasks of personality therapy is to promote the individuation process—or the full growth and unfolding of the personality. Jung firmly believed that the total personality must be given an opportunity to flourish; consciousness should be expanded to include all these various aspects. We sometimes hear it said that a particular person is a total person. The implication is that the individual is complete, possessing, in a balanced manner, everything that is required to be a fully developed human being. Jung sought to promote this kind of wholeness and completeness in personality by helping the patient experience his total personality.

The first step was to know the persona, which is the mask we wear to successfully adapt to our various external conditions. A person should be quite clear about the various roles he performs, and the difference between these and the more personal aspects of his nature—his selfish tendencies, his moods, his personal aspirations. It is not easy to separate our social roles from the rest of personality because these roles are usually quite flattering. Yet this is an essential step in the process of becoming an individuated personality.

The next step in self-exploration is the discovery of the shadow, the term Jung uses to cover our negative behaviors, our selfish impulses and drives, and the worst elements of our nature. As we have noted, we know some of our faults; but obviously many of them are kept out of awareness because they are quite opposed to the persona, the social mask we wear. Painful as it may be, the knowledge of shadow elements in our personality can increase the breadth and integration of personality. Further, if we know them, we can deal with our faults and selfish tendencies.

As one becomes aware of his social personality and shadow behaviors, the next step is to uncover and integrate into the conscious personality of the opposite-sex traits. It may seem strange to say that we need to become aware of our opposite-sex traits; but Jung was convinced that the total personality of individuals of both sexes could only be complete when this was accomplished. He believed that every man has feminine traits in personality make-up which are a part of his very nature. Likewise, every woman has masculine traits. Normally, everyone strives to perfect the persona, the feminine or masculine social role, because it enables one to adapt to the external world; but the persona qualities are in conflict with the unconscious and weak traits of the opposite sex. Jung called the feminine traits in a man the anima traits, and the masculine traits in a woman, the animus traits. Masculine and feminine traits complement each other, if there is a proper balance within the individual and between the sexes. Thus Jung believed that the masculine ego and persona are tempered by feminine qualities, such as sensitivity to others and tender emotions, when a man integrates his anima traits into consciousness. He also believed that the feminine ego and persona are tempered by masculine traits—steadfastness and rationality, for example— as a woman gains awareness of animus traits within her consciousness. The young man who aspires to live up to the image of masculinity may develop a one-sided ego; but if he integrates into his conscious ego his feminine traits, he becomes much more capable of a broader range of human contacts. Likewise, the developing woman who aspires to fulfill the feminine image may also develop in a one-sided manner, but she too becomes a more complete person by acknowledging and expressing her masculine qualities.

As more and more of the personality make-up is made conscious, the true center of personality begins to emerge. Jung called this the self. Selfhood is not an automatic unfolding process but is attained through self-exploration, as noted above.

The Levels of Consciousness

We are all aware of the ebb and flow of consciousness and of the ego which we experience as the subject and object of our experiences. There is a continuous inflow of sensory information. External events set off chains of ideas and feelings. Most people think that this is all there is to the human psyche. But investigators, such as Freud, found much more. He studied the unconscious mind extensively because he found that disorders of personality were often due to unconscious experiences. A painful experience in childhood might be forgotten, for all practical purposes, but it lives on in the unconscious to disrupt behavior. For example, a young girl who had been sexually assaulted might have unexplainable difficulty with sexual feelings and behavior as an adult.

Jung was influenced by Freud's view of the unconscious. He accepted this concept of the unconscious; but he also came to believe that there was a deeper layer, which he called the collective unconscious. The example of the sexually assaulted girl illustrates what Jung called the personal unconscious, because it is a level of the unconscious acquired through personal experiences. In contrast to the personal unconscious, Jung believes that the collective unconscious is inherited. The personal unconscious is acquired in the lifetime of the individual. It consists primarily of unacceptable thoughts and urges, but it also harbors repressed memories of painful early experiences. By contrast, the collective unconscious is inherited: it provides the potentiality for universal images of human experiences, and these take individual form in each person through encounters with the real world.

The Collective Unconscious.   Jung was impressed with the similarity of myths and ceremonial practices throughout the world.

People who had no connection with each other, removed in time and distance, had the same characters in their legends, the same themes, and even the same rituals. Where did these come from? Jung concluded that they were predispositions existing in the psyche of man, which would emerge when certain events took place. Giving birth is certainly a significant event in the life of a woman and her community, and many ceremonies to honor and give meaning to the event developed. These ceremonies are identical in many different parts of the world. The same could be said of the other major events of life and death.

Complexes

As we have noted, we are not always aware of everything that influences us. Jung maintained that the personal unconscious, which contains many unpleasant, emotionally charged ideas, may disrupt the work of the ego. Jung introduced the notion of a complex, which is an elaboration of Freud's notion of repression, to cover a relatively autonomous unconscious system of ideas and feelings. A complex is very much like an independent subpersonality that can easily take over the ego, or get in the way of the powers of the ego. For instance, a person with an inferiority complex interprets everything according to his personal inferiority. He may minimize evidence that goes against his complex of inferiority. The person does not have a complex, but rather, as Jung pointed out, the complex has him. The person who has a success complex always thinks about, worries over, and values achievement. There are so many things that are tied or linked to the success complex that practically everything sets it off. He can hardly talk about anything else except making more money, or working out a good deal, or developing a new project. The ego, which is dominated by one or more complexes, is hampered in its function as the coordinator of the personality. Some people's lives are dominated by a few highly intense and pervasive complexes, and all their thoughts circle about these. Complexes must be brought to consciousness, so that they can be reduced in intensity. The ego under the influence of a complex is a puppet. In general, complexes make for a lopsided personality.

Archetypes

If we observe the course of development of an infant, it becomes quite evident that practically everything he does is the
product of learning. Except for a few basic reflexes and drives, the
original equipment is primarily potential for behavior. Each
person inherits tendencies or predispositions for certain types of
learning that are characteristic of the species and also unique to
that individual. Given no opportunity to learn, the human would
remain in a highly primitive state. Several outstanding thinkers,
including Aristotle, argued that the mind is like a wax tablet on
which experiences make impressions. The conscious mind, as
Freud observed, is quite limited in its immediate span; but he
argued for an acquired unconscious which is the storehouse for the
conscious mind.

Jung argued that, although we are not born with already formed
ideas, we are born with tendencies to have certain experiences. The
brain is a complex organ with its own evolved structures. He
believed that significant human experiences, often repeated, create
dispositions to have images of those experiences, and that these
dispositions are inherited. We inherit certain latent images that will
be activated, or filled in, when we encounter real experiences. For
example, think of the perfect mother. There are only a limited
number of images that fit the mother—protector, spiritual guide,
a witch-like creature, the embodiment of wisdom. Which of these
becomes the dominant image depends on actual experiences. One
of them will be activated. The collective unconscious contains
latent images of typical human situations—death, birth, feminin-
ity, masculinity, growth—and of significant figures—God, the
devil, mother, the wise old man. Take another example which
further elaborates the nature of archetypes: One's conception of
death may be quite varied. One person may see it as complete
annihilation and the end of everything. Another conceives of it as
a sleep-like state, a transition to immortal life. Death has been
depicted as a dark stranger that comes like a thief in the night. No
one teaches us these conceptions or images. Likewise, the image of
God varies from person to person: One experiences the deity as a
powerful judge who has full control, and is to be feared. Another

experiences the deity as a providential father who tempers justice with mercy. The world and the psyche of primitive people were dominated with gods and demons. Jung asked where they came from, and his answer was: from man's collective unconscious. We inherit predispositions to have certain fears—such as fear of the dark, of snakes, or of the devil. These are a part of our unconscious potential at birth and our actual learning experiences will activate these original images.

The contents of the collective unconscious exist as tendencies, preformed *patterns* for personal behavior. Certain experiences are easy to have because there is already a predisposition to have them. Jung points out that more archetypes will be activated as one's experience broadens. A person who has a very dominant father may perceive all men in authority as tyrants, but having experience with many men in authority increases the number of images that one may use in dealing with authorities.

We may see the operation of archetypes most directly in children. For the child, images of things and people are highly tinged with the fantastic and the magical. The child believes that his father is all-powerful, or all-knowing. The child stands in awe of the doctor, the policeman, the teacher, the minister. These important figures are not seen as human beings with frailties and shortcomings, but according to archetypal forms—forms which can be found all over the world, both now and in the historical past.

Our images help us to interpret events, but if these images are distorted, either we may fail to see things that are there, or we may see things that are not there. The child's images, dominated as they are by archetypes, must be modified so that they correspond to the real events and people in his environment. A person who trembles before any authority figure, or one who deifies members of the opposite sex, will not behave adaptively and effectively because his images of these people are distorted. For example, one who misperceives members of the opposite sex may actually fall in love with his image of the person rather than with the real person. This can only lead to serious error. We must always be on guard to check our images against reality. Some people are convinced that practically everyone else is superior and endowed with unusual charm, capabilities, and desirable traits. The distorted image comes between the ego and the external object and causes a misinterpretation; it is clear that in a sense, then, an archetype may be seen as a complex, since it can, like a complex, influence the ego.

The archetype should be considered a real image that a person has, not a mysterious and abstract entity. Our images are often strong motive forces and generate much behavior. Consider the many monuments—pyramids, cathedrals, churches, mosques, temples—that have been erected in fear or homage to a deity. These buildings are nonfunctional in any practical sense, but they are symbolic expressions of a powerful archetype, a real image in the life of people.

Many things are outside the realm of man's knowledge—the meaning of life, the necessity of death, birth, pain, and natural disasters. Images of these have led to ceremonies, customs, and a variety of symbols. Man's symbolic practices play an essential part in living, and help man to cope with the condition of human existence. To do away with such symbols leaves the mysteries of life without any kind of response. Jung held that this elimination of a proper channel for response is very dangerous, and that it is one of the causes of such unhappiness today.

Attitudes and Functions

To understand Jung's fully developed person, we need to look at his ideas on psychological types. He divided people into extroverts and introverts, depending on the manner in which psychic energy is directed. The extrovert is oriented to objects, events, and people; the introvert is oriented toward his own subjective or psychological states. In addition to these general postures or attitudes toward life, Jung also distinguished four psychological functions—thinking, feeling, sensing, and intuiting. The thinking type is concerned about the meaning of things, system, and order. The feeling type is acutely aware of the value of things. The sensing type strives to have a complete picture of things as they are. The intuitive type is sensitive to the possibilities that people and things have. Ideally, these attitudes and functions should support and complement each other. This brief account hardly does justice to this important topic. The important thing is that we inherit tendencies to follow a particular orientation and function, that is, an extroverted or introverted orientation, thinking rather than feeling. To attain individuation, we must be on guard not to overemphasize these natural tendencies, but to allow all aspects of the personality to be conscious and expressed. The naturally extroverted person should express his introverted requirements by paying attention to his inner life. Likewise, the person who functions predominantly according to the feeling mode should strengthen and express his intellectual functions to balance this one-sided tendency.

Abnormal Types

Jung speaks of abnormality in a number of ways. He generally accepts the notion of abnormality as excess or deficiency of functioning. But he is also concerned with imbalance among the various components of personality. He is insistent that none of the systems of the personality be overemphasized at the expense of the other systems. If the persona is too powerful, the person may be like a hollow shell. If the shadow is dominant, the person may be violent and criminal. If the anima of a man is overemphasized, the person may become perverted. If the animus of a woman is not properly expressed, she may be argumentative and excessively competitive with men. If a person is extremely extroverted or introverted, his behavior may be exaggerated and inappropriate in many situations. A person who stresses thinking over the other functions is also cutting off vital forces in his personality. Likewise, the person who is ruled by his feelings and emotions may make many irrational judgments and decisions. Not dealing adequately with archetypal images may cause a variety of problems. Jung believed that we have an inborn need to respond to the mysteries of life such as the worship of a deity, the requirement of a mother figure, and the respect for power. As a result of an untempered archetype, a man may easily fall in love because he sees any woman who makes an impression as a goddess. His image of woman gets in the way of any realistic perception of a particular woman. It should be noted that the type of abnormality with which Jung was most concerned was the lack of unity and integration in personality.

The Persona and Inflation

One of the most important archetypes is one's image of being a social being. This archetype helps us to form an image of ourselves as a member of the various groups with which we are associated. One's persona serves as a guide to help us live and work with others. But one may go too far in the development of his persona, his social personality. One may overidentify with the persona. In this sense, the term overidentification means that the ego becomes the social role the person assumes. A doctor may so identify with his role that he does not know how to be a husband to his wife, a son to his mother, and a father to his children. He cannot be himself in any setting because he continually wears his role as a doctor. In contrast, many people find that they can "put on" a role, just as they dress in a certain way for work. They shed this role, which serves them well in their vocation, when they are with their friends or at home. In this sense, one deliberately cultivates a functional persona, but is not dominated by it. Taking a role too seriously may cause the condition known as inflation, which is an overvaluation of the ego which itself is overidentified with the persona. In such an instance, the person needs constant demonstrations of his worth. He is quite vulnerable to threat because his whole psychological being depends on the continual feeding of the ego. Furthermore, vital aspects of personality are blocked because they threaten the persona.

The Harmful Effects of the Shadow

The evil aspects of man, both as individuals and as groups, are quite evident. Violent crime and wars are all around us. We are daily appalled by the viciousness of human aggression. The evil tendencies in all of us take many subtle forms. Parents can be cruel and irrational with children. Some teachers are sadistic with their pupils. Those in authority often needlessly cause their subordinates pain and sorrow, and all of us occasionally play out our negative emotions on others. We tend to deny such unpleasant things; and not only do we try to prevent others from knowing them, but we also block them from our own awareness by pushing them into the unconscious, where they become a part of the shadow. However, these shadow elements of personality often tyrannize the ego, and consequently we behave in nasty and anti-social ways—often without even knowing it. A resulting paradox is that sometimes the very people who have a high regard for themselves are vicious and ill-tempered without knowing it: Their shadow takes over their ego because they have so vigorously denied its existence.

The person may have been brought up with the idea that impulses and strong emotions are unbecoming to a mature adult. As a consequence, these may be overcontrolled. They become a part of the shadow in personality. Just as overidentifying with the persona role limits and misshapes the ego, so does cutting off the impulses and emotions. The ego is hampered, then, by both the persona and the shadow. As the power of these elements is lessened, the ego increases in freedom.

Harmful Effects of the Anima and Animus

In order to understand our nature fully, Jung believed that we had to become aware of the qualities of the opposite sex which are in each of us. In becoming either male or female, the opposite-sex genes are not lost. They produce, both physically and psychologically, characteristics of the opposite sex. For example, the personalities of the two sexes are quite similar in infancy and early childhood. Yet the traits of the opposite sex in us can soon begin to create problems. For one thing, these opposite-sex traits are quite opposed to the persona. A growing boy is very concerned about not being like girls; and girls generally, at least until recently, are also sensitive to what is considered masculine behavior. Jung held to a clear difference between masculine and feminine psychology. He realized that although culture may promote certain roles for the sexes, these roles may be contrary to the basic nature of the sexes. We must learn that there is nothing sacred about cultural expectations: Many personality therapists have seen the casualties resulting from overidentification with cultural roles in their consultant chambers.

Jung thought that masculine psychology stresses unemotionality, a problem orientation to life, aggressiveness, and an external orientation with competence and mastery as major goals. On the other hand, he thought that feminine psychology stresses emotionality, warm human contacts, mothering and protectiveness, and a concern with the inner life. Jung not only distinguished between masculine and feminine traits; he also distinguished between desirable and undesirable masculine and feminine traits. The persona, as it relates to masculine and feminine identity, is maladaptive. In extreme form, man is brutish, savage, and crude, while woman in extreme form is fickle, volatile, and neurotic. Yet such extreme traits can be made functional by the tempering influence of the opposite qualities. A brutish man becomes a gentleman by allowing his anima traits expression. We might think of anima as animation, the emotional and feeling aspect of personality. The supermasculine role is given animation by the feminine traits of sociability, spontaneity, and tender care for loved ones. Likewise, the woman's psyche is balanced by masculine traits. Because of these traits, she is able to be decisive, problem-oriented, and autonomous in her dealings with people. The animus traits give stability and direction to her life. Animus resembles animosity: One who is capable of animosity can be assertive in her behavior. We may be flattered that our good-natured pet dog makes the world over us, but if that same dog evidenced the anger that could tear us to pieces, its good-natured attentions would be still more appreciated. The anima traits complete the masculine psyche, and the animus traits make the woman a complete person.

Jung has made a unique contribution regarding masculine and feminine archetypes. It will be recalled that archetypes are images that represent typical human situations and figures. The various images of women define the different roles which women have played in the lives of men. A man may have one of these images, and he deals with women through its influence. The images are both positive and negative. Here are some of the typical images that men have had of women: the virgin, the eternal mother, the witch, the harlot, the temptress, the spiritual guide. A man may view and react to women exclusively in terms of one of these archetypes rather than as the total people they really are. All men have these various images of women as latent predispositions. The particular image which emerges depends upon early experience with women and girls—mother, sisters, early childhood crushes, and so forth. Once an archetype is activated by real experience, it becomes a stereotype which is difficult to change; but having several images of women increases the man's ability to relate with women. The objective is to perceive a woman more as she is rather than in accordance with a stereotype.

Just as the anima of a man contributes to the images a particular man has of women, the animus of a woman also contributes to the images she has of men. There have been many roles that men have played in the life of women. The particular image depends on early experiences with men and boys—father, brothers, and sweethearts. Once the image of man is formed in the psyche of a girl, it persists as an influence in her dealings with men. She may perceive a man as an adventurer, a seducer, a rapist, a protector, a father image, or as a knight errant who will sweep her off her feet. Any particular man who makes an impression on her is judged according to one of these images. Her relationships with men may be seriously disturbed. She may fall head-over-heels in love with a particular man, only to find that he turns out to be totally different from her first impressions of him. Of course, her first impression was formed primarily under the domination of the masculine archetype. Men and women who have difficulty knowing and responding to the opposite sex usually have not dealt adequately with their archetypes of the other sex. Their response is more appropriate to the universal image than to the real people they encounter. Thus each person should allow his full nature, which includes both masculine and feminine traits, to be expressed and he should also broaden his experiences with members of the opposite sex so that he forms functional images which depict real people, not archetypes.

IDEAL PERSONALITY AND LIVING

Achievement of Selfhood

Jung contrasted the ego, which is essentially the center of the persona, with the self, which is an achievement of the middle years of life. The self does not simply unfold, but requires great effort to attain; and many do not get beyond the ego and the persona level of functioning.

In the first half of life, Jung believed, personality development is primarily determined by the requirements of the culture and also by the instincts, both of which are extremely powerful during this period. The growing child invests his psychological energy in learning the many skills and traits that enable him to make adjustments to his world. With the arrival of adolescence, the sex drive intensifies, and many new problems emerge. Preparation for adult living is quite arduous. It is often a bitter struggle for one to learn about himself and about all the things that must be done to assume the adult status. Expectations are often set too high, and the person experiences much frustration and defeat. The young person wants desperately to find peace of mind and happiness, yet his life is anything but tranquil and full of joy. Each step he takes is painful, and competition is everywhere. Many people find that nothing they consider worthwhile comes without a struggle. By the middle of life, many of these struggles begin to subside. By then one has either achieved much of what he set out to do or he has learned to accept his place in life. Jung believed that during this period, psychological energy makes a radical shift: It is turned inward to more personal concerns. The middle-aged person becomes increasingly concerned about the meaning of his life, and about what lies in store for the remainder of life.

Repeatedly, Jung found, in his middle-aged patients, a sense of dissatisfaction and discouragement. Life seemed to have lost its meaning. Many of his patients in their late thirties and forties, although they were highly successful in cultural terms, no longer found their lives meaningful. They seemed to be searching for a new direction in life. They were weary of their sham existence, of their pretense of happiness and importance.

Jung advised his patients to try new ways of expressing themselves. He encouraged them to take up a hobby, such as a musical instrument, painting, writing, and even working with their hands in building things. Jung himself loved sculpting and constructing things. He found these activities to be highly satisfying and relaxing. They were a diversion from his work and his writing. He was insistent about the importance of expressing the primitive aspects of our natures. Too many people, he believed, cut themselves off from their real nature. Although civilization emphasizes rationality, the nonrational in man requires an adequate outlet, or the whole psyche will be out of balance.

Jung believed that the major problems and mysteries of life have not yet been solved, despite the amazing achievements of science. Whereas primitive people reacted to them through their rituals, ceremonies, and symbolic practices, the sophisticated person may relegate all that to superstition and ignorance. But the unknowns are as much a part of the sophisticate's life as they were for the uncivilized. We also need symbols to express our archetypes, and although the old ones may no longer suffice, we need to find some that do.

Working Toward Individuation

Jung held that one can participate in the individuation process by attempting to listen to one's unconscious promptings. One should not be afraid to go off alone and simply attend to spontaneous thoughts and feelings. Jung believed that our unconscious contains the wisdom of the ages; and that we can draw upon this fund of knowledge if we take note of our dreams, if we let ideas come to us from within, and if, in general, we pay attention to our subjective life. Individuation means an expansion of consciousness, so that all aspects of the psyche are experienced. Certainly, we need to perfect our persona, and differentiate it as much as possible, in order to deal effectively with our various social relationships. But our shadow also gives vitality and spontaneity to behavior. We should be aware of and find expression for our impulses and emotions. They are vital forces that give depth to living. The most dangerous forces in our nature are those which are not perceived consciously, and which are not under control. As the person attains fullness, the ego gives way to the self, the new center of personality. The self then allows all aspects of the personality expression.

The self can find ways of bringing together the conflicting systems. The shadow and persona represent opposites in personality; but the self can harmonize our roles with our personal desires and feelings. Both aspects may require some moderation, but the result is a sense of wholeness and integration. The opposite-sex traits can also be experienced and expressed in a balanced manner with the shadow and persona. The total blending gets rid of one-sidedness. We have already mentioned the necessity to balance extroversion and introversion and the four functions of thinking, feeling, sensing, and intuiting. Each aspect adds an important dimension to the total personality.

Self-Discovery

In his autobiography, Jung describes the personality as being vast and mysterious. One's inner world is like the universe. Jung believed that the greatest adventure of life was the exploration of this inner world. The search can be a lifelong project because each period of life is accompanied by many changes in the external environment, but more importantly within the personality itself. One can derive great excitement and joy from being a participant in this growth. One of our most cherished attributes is self-reflection, the ability to observe and contemplate our own inner workings. The greatest joy of life for Jung was self-exploration.

Many people are afraid to look within themselves. All that seems desirable is external—to be entertained, to be doing something exciting, stimulating, and drive-satisfying. However, the individuation process can become evident to us only through self-reflection. As pleasurable as this is in itself, a still greater pleasure is to promote one's growth processes actively through the use of all one's abilities. Jung himself devoted most of his life to studying the manifestations of the unconscious mind, his own included.

The Principle of Transcendence

As personality grows, it becomes more complex. New traits and capabilities increase the adaptive potential of the individual; but these also cause conflicts, as the various systems which make up personality compete. The systems compete with each other for the existing psychic energy. Consider the following oppositions which may develop. The persona attempts to influence the ego by displaying to it the many benefits of social success. On the other hand, the shadow draws the attention of the ego to basic personal strivings—to drive satisfaction and to appetite indulgence. It may flood the ego with negative emotions such as hate, resentment, and antisocial impulses. The anima traits of a man may pressure the ego toward tenderness, creativity, sentimentality, and love; but these compete with his persona. The animus traits of a woman may cause her to question her feminine roles, and prompt the ego to compete with men.

These opposing tendencies are natural in man; thus it requires a highly developed personality, one in which selfhood has been attained, to resolve the conflicts. As the person becomes fully aware of himself, greater control becomes possible. The union of opposites is a high level function of the self. We noted earlier that this transcendent function of the self involves moderation, blending, and creative use of abilities. Opposite traits are turned into complementary traits, and these support rather than compete with one another. Instead of being a fawning, self-degrading employee, one accepts himself as a cooperative worker, but also as a person who is self-assertive and self-respecting. One might display both strength and courage in his everyday dealings, but also have compassion and concern for others. A woman may be femininely appealing, but also self-assured and capable in meeting the requirements of living.

Jung makes an interesting observation with respect to conflicts. A person who has many conflicts with others may be experiencing conflicts within himself—conflicts between his own opposing tendencies and traits. A man who is creating a great deal of friction with others may be manifesting his own inner conflict between his persona and anima nature. A woman who cannot get along with her superiors may be reflecting her own conflict between her animus and persona. Her unrecognized masculine tendencies conflict with her feminine identity. In both instances, the union of opposites within will lessen the conflicts without.

Portrait of Jung's Individuated Person

The general impression of the individuated personality is that he is both natural and highly complex. The person has transcended the natural oppositions by harmonizing his opposing qualities. There is also a profound inner life, a life of continual discovery. Jung's ideal is deeply involved with self-experiencing. He is philosophical, and yearns to appreciate and participate in shaping his outer and inner worlds. He is able to face unknowns with awe, wonder, and acceptance. He is social and playful, serious and creative, rational and emotional; but his greatest asset is his own self-appreciation. He is at peace with himself—an integrated, balanced, fully developed, and fully functioning personality. Jung's individuated personality would certainly meet the highest ideals of humanness.

EGO SOCIAL MODELS: RATIONAL AND SOCIAL MAN

II

Those who propose an idea that contradicts a prevailing one sometimes tend to exaggerate its importance. Freud and Jung reacted to the prevailing view of man as rational and as being fully conscious and capable of making free choices by demonstrating the existence of powerful unconscious urges and irrational thinking. They so convincingly dramatized man's irrationality and primitive nature that man's consciousness and the ego itself were viewed as playing a relatively minor role. Freud viewed the ego merely as the servant of basic unconscious urges. The role of culture and the immediate environment also appeared to some personality scientists to be inadequately treated by Freud and Jung, who believed that basic needs were much more important than the environment. One's immediate home atmosphere might be crucial in shaping personality; but once personality was formed, Freud believed it did not change essentially.

It became apparent that a new approach was necessary to restore the rightful place of the ego and of social and cultural influences. Erik Erikson proposed the view that personality development was primarily the growth of the ego as the person confronts the major tasks of life. Each success strengthens the ego in an important way. Alfred Adler related the growth of the ego to sociocultural conditions. He maintained that man is capable of self-direction and of controlling his own destiny, and that the only normal existence for man can take place in social settings such as the family, the community, or a work setting. Social interest keeps man from becoming neurotic. Social concerns cut across everything a person does. Karen Horney also stressed the growth of the ego or self. She viewed abnormality primarily as being the loss of contact with the real self and the formation, instead, of an unreal and glamorous self. Her objective was to bring the person back to his real self. For Horney, the major problems of life were conflicts involving other people. She viewed social needs and environmental circumstances as critical in personality formation and functioning. We will next consider the views of these ego-social personality scientists.

The Eight Great
Tasks of Life:
Erik Erikson

4

Erik Erikson was born in Frankfort, Germany, in 1902. The young Erikson appeared to be destined for a career in art; but a school friend helped to change all that by encouraging him to come for training in psychoanalysis in a school for lay psychoanalysts in Vienna. Unlike the typical psychoanalyst, he did not have medical training; in fact, he did not even have a college degree. Despite his lack of formal training, he has taught in several medical schools, including Harvard Medical School. He has distinguished himself as a pioneer in child psychiatry, and has written several important works in this field. Furthermore, he has written two highly acclaimed psychohistorical analyses; one dealing with the life of Mahatma Gandhi and the other with Martin Luther.

Erikson has promoted the interesting method of studying personality by tracing its growth. Observing the course of changes which take place in personality can help us to understand what is normal as well as abnormal growth; and we can hope to promote in ourselves the best possible development when we know what the best behaviors for effective living are.

Erikson's study of the developing person convinced him that we go through fairly distinct stages of personality growth. In a real sense, we become a different person in each stage of life. All you have to do to see this point is to look back at yourself five or ten years ago. Consider the difference between what you were at ten years of age and what you are now. Your total life style is different: This includes marked changes in physical size, a whole new set of responsibilities, different goals, and new frustrations. Erikson delineates eight distinct periods of the life cycle; thus, he believes that personality changes all through life. Erikson sees one major problem in each of the eight periods that has to be met successfully. If the task is accomplished when it is pertinent, the ego is strengthened. If a certain major task of the ego is not achieved, the person not only has difficulties during that particular period, but the next stage of life is still more difficult. The person then has a new problem as well as the preceding difficulties. Erikson believes that the child must develop a basic sense of trust in his environment because he is totally dependent on others for his very survival. But all through life we are dependent upon our environment, which of course includes people. Because we do not have, and can never have, full control of things, we must have faith and trust. A distrusting person lives a highly stressful life. Having a basic sense of trust or mistrust cuts across practically everything we do.

As the child grows up, he must begin doing things for himself: He must become independent or autonomous. Excessive difficulty in making decisions, resolving conflicts, and resisting distraction are indications that an adult has not achieved a sense of autonomy. One way to look at Erikson's ego accomplishments is as a model of attributes which can foster the good life, and which we can strive to promote in ourselves.

BASIC CONCEPTS AND PRINCIPLES

You and Your Environment

We know that each person has an individual nature which is determined by his inheritance. At the same time, however, we are born into a certain cultural and geographical setting. We are all exposed to certain influences, such as climate, types of foods, language, and, depending upon the immediate circumstances of our class, certain educational and home conditions. Even the achievements of a people depend to some extent on the climate: Those cultures from the temperate zone have evolved more technologically than have cultures from the climatic extremes.

Erikson became interested in the Sioux Indians of South Dakota, and lived among them for several months. The Sioux were a nomadic group who followed the migration of the buffalo, their major food. Being a nomadic people, they had to work closely together because they did not store things. Sharing and concern for one another were high priorities, because survival was a group affair. How different this is from the values of Western cultures, which stress individual accomplishment and competition! Everyone is encouraged to be the best, and to gain a place of superiority over others. We are speaking primarily of the so-called middle-class values. Yet Erikson found that it was difficult to get the young Sioux to compete with each other. For instance, when they played football, they did not keep score because no one wanted to humiliate the loser. This type of thinking seems abnormal to many of us because our total orientation to life is competitive. Competition is not a defining characteristic of mankind; rather, it is culturally established.

A Crisis, or Turning Point

Erikson holds that each stage of life is centered about a crisis; he does not mean a catastrophe or an overwhelming stress, but, rather, a turning point. A major new task must be confronted, and the way that it is handled will affect the total life style of the person. The child of about five or six is faced with the task of leaving his relatively sheltered home environment to begin his long period at school. This is a major turning point in the life of the child, requiring a totally new orientation to life. What about the major change that occurs when formal education is finished, and the person has to face the requirements of adult living? Failures are conspicuous in each of these periods of life.

No Permanent Solutions

As we have noted, each period of life confronts the ego with a major task; but all the tasks are present in some form in all the periods of the life cycle. For instance, we are always faced with the conflict between trusting or mistrusting people, trusting or mistrusting our circumstances, and trusting or mistrusting the unknown future. In the same way, both the child and the elderly person are concerned about a sense of personal identity; but the problem—the identity crisis—becomes critical in late adolescence and early adulthood.

The Best Approach to the Future

As you survey the future, you may be afraid of not being able to handle the increased responsibilities. Being grown-up is an ideal for the young person, but being an adult can produce feelings of insecurity and anxiety. When one has to go on his own, he enjoys the many benefits of independence, but he must also suffer the consequences of his failures. Erikson would advise the young person to concentrate on doing the best job possible in the immediate circumstances as the best means of preparing for future changes. You will be helped by your own growing resources. When the time comes to go to work, to get married, to bring up a family, or to accept the changes that come with ageing, you will be assisted by the natural unfolding of your potential to change. The changes are remarkable and you can count on your own inner resources if you meet the major task of each period of life head-on and work to acquire the necessary skills and attitudes to accomplish that task.

NORMAL AND ABNORMAL EGO DEVELOPMENT

Erikson was very much impressed with the role of the ego as it grows and increases in strength. The ego stands between our needs and the external environment; the kind of life we lead depends on the capabilities of the ego. We will consider Erikson's views on both normal and abnormal ego development.

Trust Versus Mistrust

Erikson holds that a sense of trust that all will go well is not only essential for the helpless infant but for all of us. We are often faced with unknowns, partial evidence, and even conflicting information; yet we must make decisions and do the best we can. We all know someone who died young, or someone who has an incurable disease: These things could happen to us. Yet thinking about such possibilities does not really add anything to life. In fact, such thinking can only hold us back and interfere with our constructive forces. A person with a sense of trust can be optimistic and hope for a better tomorrow. Hope refers to positive expectations in the absence of direct evidence. Since we do not know the hazards of the future, we can be either pessimistic or optimistic. The trusting person cultivates the virtue of hope, while the mistrusting person lives with fear and insecurity. Fear is a crippling emotion because it holds the person back from doing things. It is rather self-evident that a person who trusts his environment and himself is much better off than the one who is suspicious of everyone and everything, and who lacks self-confidence.

Autonomy Versus Shame and Doubt

Between the ages of one and three, the child is expected to become less dependent on his parents, and to begin controlling his natural urges. He is expected to eat when others do, and to gain eventual control over his elimination requirements. Control means being capable of tolerating tension. It also requires will power and courage to do things for oneself. A sense of autonomy means that one is willing to stand on his own feet and develop the courage to take responsibility for himself. The ordinary person has to be courageous, not in the sense that a fighter or hero is daring or brave; rather, the persistence in daily accomplishment. We are expected to carry on even when we have been hurt, or have suffered failure, or are simply tired of the routine. We must have the courage to break with the past, to meet change with flexibility, and to go our own way even in the face of opposition from others. The long period of childhood may engender in us a feeling of being small and unworthy. Parents sometimes use shame as a means of getting their children to do certain things. "What will grandmother think of you now?" Often, the child has to resort to underhanded means to get what he wants; he may be caught at it, and then be made to feel petty and unworthy of his parents' love. A sense of shame means that the person feels small and unlovable. My sense of autonomy tells me that I have as much right to be here as anyone else. It is essential that we outgrow the feeling of smallness that is so strong in childhood.

The autonomous person minimizes feelings of shame and self-doubt because he has worked out his own values, and because he attempts to carry them out through his behavior. He judges himself according to his success or failure in living up to his own values, and he is not swayed by the good or bad opinion of others. Autonomy requires the courage of self-conviction.

Initiative Versus Guilt

Shame is a form of self-consciousness that results from uncertainty regarding the good opinion of other people. It takes such forms as embarrassment, feeling conspicuous, and feeling different from others. Guilt, on the other hand, is felt as a violation of conscience, a failure to live up to one's own standards. The child of three to six years of age is told what is considered right and wrong behavior, and gradually these prescriptions of conduct are made a part of conscience. The child is held responsible for doing certain things and avoiding others. At first the standards are external to the child and their violation may be punished by making the child feel shame. Eventually we make these standards our own and judge ourselves according to whether or not we live up to them.

To take initiative means to pursue the satisfaction of our needs and wants actively; but this is sometimes met with punishment and failure. The child is placed in a conflict between trying to satisfy his needs and wants and being threatened by punishment if he goes too far or does the wrong thing. Punishment may cause a sense of guilt, which holds the person back from asserting himself. Guilt is also a blocking force in personality, and causes feelings of unworthiness. To take risks and to make mistakes are part of the business of living. To be absolutely secure and without guilt, one may simply restrict his needs to practically nothing; but then his life becomes meaningless and minimal. A sense of initiative supports a vigorous approach to living: The person aggressively seeks and strives for what he needs and wants.

Industry Versus Inferiority

The child of school age is expected to learn certain skills and is judged rather harshly if he fails. Basic skills are essential to all aspects of living: from pursuing a vocation to getting along with people. Skills are valuable possessions, and we should strive to perfect them, and, above all, to value them. We have a drive to experience success, and to be good at what we do; but unfortunately, many people who might otherwise experience a sound sense of industry actually feel inferior because they constantly compare their skills and achievements with those of others who are better. We may judge ourselves by glamorous cultural standards which are really attained by only a few. We should be bold enough to set our own objectives and standards. Your own skills should be valued, irrespective of what others do. Success experiences need not be earthshaking to be satisfying, if one takes the proper attitude. Inferiority is one of our major problems in life, and we can overcome it by cultivating skills and talents. For man, work is one of the most gratifying activities, because it can meet many of our basic needs.

Identity Versus Role Confusion

We are always struggling with the question of identity. Am I really a decent person who is concerned about others, or am I most concerned about myself? Am I an extrovert or an introvert, hardworking or lazy, and so forth? Many things come together in early adulthood: We are expected to be independent, to follow some kind of vocation, to get married, and to support a family. These are big decisions, and they all come at the same time. The young person may feel divided and uncertain. He may have many conflicts about the type of person he is and wants to become. Erikson speaks of attaining and preserving a stable sense of identity, a core ego role that seems to fit us. In order to hope to attain a sense of identity in early adulthood, one must have achieved a sense of trust, of autonomy, of initiative, and of industry. Self-consciousness is acute during the period when identity is a major problem for the person. There is confusion about abilities, roles, values, and vocation. The person knows that he has some control over his own life—his preferences, goals, and aspirations—but there is much uncertainty regarding which of these is truly his own. We all have the tasks of assembling and bringing together many previous roles, expectations, talents, aptitudes, skills, defenses, and coping devices. One strives to become a stable and identifiable person with a particular style of life. Lack of a sense of identity leads to role confusion. The person simply cannot find himself, and does not know who he really is. He tries out different roles, but none seem to fit him. He feels chaos within himself, and others find him difficult to know and understand because he is so changeable. We need to establish a sense of self-sufficiency and worth, so that we are essentially self-accepting.

Intimacy Versus Isolation

The ability to form an abiding and intimate relationship requires the possession of certain ego strengths. A sense of trust is necessary in order to allow the other person to be himself. Autonomy is essential because loving concern demands sacrifice and giving. Initiative is required to add the extra touches of spontaneity. A firm sense of identity is a key ingredient because one must have a stable ego role in order to give and to receive love. Some of the most distinctively human emotions, such as empathy, sympathy, compassion, and mutual respect, are brought together in an intimate relationship. The normal person needs the support of other humans, and when one lacks this he experiences a sense of isolation and aloneness. The person who experiences a sense of isolation feels misunderstood and unacceptable even to himself.

Generativity Versus Stagnation

Erikson believes that the period of life which spans the years from 25 to 50 can be highly productive and fulfilling because one has reached his peak in many ways. This period is potentially quite rich in need gratification. Using our abilities productively gives pleasure. The term generative means creative and productive. Stagnation comes from inability to use abilities to satisfy needs and attain goals. A sense of stagnation comes from routine living and lack of commitment to anything. Sustained productive work and abiding love are among man's greatest achievements. To make a commitment to someone or to some cause, as the existentialists hold, is one of the marks of humanness. Often, we approach a task with opposing tendencies. One part of us says "no," and resists the effort; another says "yes," and there is conflict. But conflict impedes initiative and successful performance.

We hear a good deal about commitment these days. A commitment means a definite decision to do what you set out to accomplish. A father may resist and fight his obligations. To make a commitment means that he takes his role seriously. Many students just simply drag along, and never really make a commitment to get the job done. In any case, the generative person is one who begins to produce after the long period of preparation. One uses his abilities to make life interesting.

Integrity Versus Despair

As Erikson uses the term, ego integrity means something like selfhood, or self-completion. Having gone through the various stages fairly successfully, one has accomplished most of his basic desires and met his emerging needs; thus the person is ready for death. At least, he does not face it with terror. But the one who has not lived his life well feels cheated and resentful. He may be depressed and fearful, and in Erikson's terms, he suffers from despair.

Each stage of life confronts the individual with new stresses and demands; but each stage also provides potential satisfactions not previously available. The child does not enjoy the privileges of independence and marriage, but at the same time he is more free to play and is relatively *free of responsibility.* The young adult cannot retire or pursue his hobbies as much as he pleases, but he can derive satisfaction from his work and home life. The middle-aged person cannot return to the pleasures of his childhood, but he can enjoy a sense of accomplishment and fulfillment that can only come from having met and successfully completed many of life's major tasks. Following the same line of thinking, the elderly person may either torment himself with regrets, a sense of futility, and a feeling of emptiness, or he can partake of the potential benefits of his so-called golden years. At every stage in life we can choose to lament the lost opportunities and imperfections in our lives, or we can put such fruitless thinking aside and focus on the current and future opportunities and satisfactions.

The Socialized
and Creative Person:
Alfred Adler

5

Alfred Adler (1870-1937) lived most of his life in Vienna. Just fourteen years after Freud, he went to the same medical school in Vienna. In fact, when Adler learned of Freud's work, he became so interested that he joined Freud's psychoanalytic movement. After a few years, it became apparent that his ideas were not consistent with Freud's, and eventually Adler started his own school, which he named individual psychology. His system of concepts and methods of treatment are quite popular; and one could probably find several personality therapists who follow Adler in every major city throughout the Western world.

In its broad outline, Adler's model of personality is relatively simple. For Adler, the major motivation of life is the striving to overcome inferiority and to produce a state of security. Such striving is highly individualistic. The striving for security may be so exaggerated that the person actually seeks to be superior to others. Just as there are many types of inferiority, so also there are many types of superiority—being exempted from responsibility, getting out of work, being pampered, gaining power over others, and so forth. There are also desirable and undesirable types of superiority: Criminality is unacceptable, but being a dedicated supervisor in a large corporation is praiseworthy. When the striving for superiority is blocked, one may resort to compensation, by which Adler meant a substitute outlet for superiority striving. A key concept to understand the basic striving for superiority is what Adler calls the guiding goal. Everyone has many goals, but one stands out as being the most basic. It might be something like being loved by everyone; wanting to always be the winner; being admired, feared, or respected; being financially independent; being famous; being powerful. This guiding goal fits into a style of life which is established rather early in life. The style of life integrates the type of inferiority the person experiences, the particular forms of compensation, the particular way that superiority is attained, and the specific guiding goal which is the center of the style of life. Adler rounds out his model of man with two other major concepts: the creative self and social feelings. Adler accepted man as being rational and conscious of his circumstances and himself. Adler firmly believed that man has the capacity to control his own destiny and to improve his life continually. The creative self can bring together all aspects of the personality and even lessen and eliminate undesirable aspects of the basic style of life. Man is not only conscious but also self-conscious. The principle of social interest means that every normal person has inborn social tendencies; and through encouragement and proper support, these tendencies can grow and become a major influence in the personality. Again, social interest and sentiments can moderate all the other operating principles—inferiority, compensations, striving for superiority, style of life, and creative self.

BASIC CONCEPTS AND PRINCIPLES

The Nature of Inferiority

Adler believed that man could not survive in nature because his physical attributes are inferior to many animals. Man does not have the physical strength and equipment to live a brutish exist-ence, so he had to develop his psychological apparatus as fully as possible. As individuals, we are constantly confronted with feelings of inferiority. The human spends many years in a state of subordination and dependence, and this period can set the pattern for a profound sense of inferiority. Adler pointed out that the sense of inferiority can be appreciated if one thinks of the relation-ship of midget to giant. In our lives as children, almost everyone is a giant; and for many of us, that state continues. Everyone is brighter, better off, more attractive, more socially desirable, and so on. Our perception of things may be so selective, under the force of the inferiority feelings, that we only see evidence of our inferiority in relation to others. We can always find people whose life and personal qualities are superior to ours. However it is done, we must all outgrow the sense of smallness and helplessness that we experienced so frequently as children. These thoughts and feelings exist as an inferiority complex that can easily be activated by our ongoing experiences. One gets a bad grade, and the feelings of smallness and helplessness come up. One is turned down for a date, and the same occurs. Again and again we experience the reawakening of the inferiority complex.

Compensation and Striving for Superiority

A feeling of inferiority is painful; thus it serves to motivate us to do something about it. The particular way of dealing with inferi-ority is extremely crucial in personality development and func-tioning. We can learn a great deal about ourselves and others by discovering the particular areas in which inferiority is experienced and the means which are taken to overcome it. Adler introduced the notion of compensation, by which he meant to make up for, or to cover up, a felt inferiority. Covering up a weakness helps one to feel more adequate, but the cover-up may be exaggerated. One person may compensate for his feeling of inferiority socially by a barrage of talk. He talks rapidly and loudly, and perhaps even too much. Another person with the same feeling takes the opposite approach by letting others talk and contributing as little as possible in social situations. Compensation may take many irrational forms such as overdressing, using too much makeup, trying to earn more money than others, or giving generous gifts in order to obligate others.

Adler called one type of compensation overcompensating— which means trying to excel in the very area in which the person feels most inferior. One might protest that this is a desirable quality because we should always strive to improve our condition. But the problem with overcompensation is that it often involves denial and a basic lack of self-acceptance. The person goes too far and exaggerates his efforts. He may even neglect everything else for the sake of proving that he is outstanding in the particular area. One person might sacrifice everything in pursuit of a musical career, although he encounters repeated failures and only mediocre success. A man of small stature may try to prove that he is tougher than the biggest man in his crowd by assuming an antagonistic air and being generally aggressive with others. Like so many abnormal mental devices, overcompensation is an exaggeration of a healthy striving to overcome weakness. It seems that the more the person senses his inferiority the more exaggerated his compensations and overcompensations become. Often, the difficulty is due to unrealistic goals and expectations. Even these are traceable to some basic inferiority. In the course of development, the normal person is exposed to unrealistic goals and false expectations; but these are moderated with actual experiences to conform with real abilities and possibilities.

Compensation occurs when there is a failure in attaining superiority. The compensation is a substitute outlet. A person may relate to others in a fixed manner such as bullying, or sarcasm, or argumentativeness. One gets the impression that this individual is continually trying to prove his superiority. His abnormal social manner is a compensation for his felt inferiority in social relationships.

Guiding Goal and Style of Life

Adler was very much impressed with the formation early in life of what he termed the style of life. Given the inborn nature of the child—temperament, native intelligence, constitutional tendencies and weaknesses—together with the family and social context which exist in the early period, a particular style of thinking, feeling, desiring, and acting emerges. Adler held that this style of life is formed during the first five years of life, and that despite the vast changes that take place with growth, it does not change very much. This view is quite radical, although it is not unique with Adler. Freud said it before him, and there have been many others who have said essentially the same thing. The reader need only look at his life during the past ten years: The most conspicuous thing is change—new skills, ideas, and attitudes, a greater capacity to reason and solve problems, a more mature view of things, and perhaps even significant changes in physique. To hold that the style of life is formed early seems, to me, to be a perversion of the obvious.

Life styles are characterized by such terms as optimism, pessimism, cynicism, complacency, courageousness, and cowardice. A vast amount of learning takes place after age five, especially during the school years, but the learning consists for the most part of acquiring skills and knowledge. The type of learning which takes place before age five is of a different order: It is primarily concerned with the art of living. Paradoxically, one forms a philosophy of life during infancy and early childhood, at a time when reasoning does not play much of a role. One's style of life is made up of general habits, attitudes, and traits that influence the scope of experience and behavior in the significant aspects of living. Early experiences are deeply impressed, and are generally repeated. Ordinarily, one does not change parents and in many cases family life remains fairly constant. By the time the child is five, strong habits and attitudes have been established with respect to such things as failure and disappointments; manner of relating to superiors and in dealing with people in general; matters pertaining to cleanliness, orderliness, and even work habits; and most of the basic reactions and behaviors required of a social being. Life styles are characterized by such terms as optimism, pessimism, cynicism, complacency, courageousness, and cowardice.

Guiding Goal.   An essential feature of the style of life is what Adler calls a guiding goal. We might think of the growing individual as an actor in a play. The play has a plot, which has a particular dominant theme or goal. The guiding goal is related to the type of inferiority the person experiences, and the specific manner in which the person strives to attain superiority. The youngest child in a large family might be the object of much pampering, and as a result, he might develop a style of life which contains the guiding goal of receiving unlimited attention from everyone. When we know the plot of a play, all the apparently disconnected events make sense. In the same way, when we know a person's guiding goal, much of what he does can be fitted into a coherent pattern. A selfish person displays this quality in practically everything he does—from lovemaking to making money, from his manner of worship to his friendships. If you want to discover a person's guiding goals, think of the types of things that he most values: that is, being financially independent, being attractive to members of the opposite sex, being dominant and masterful in relationships with others, always being the winner. Guiding goals may either promote or hinder successful adjustment. Being an acceptable and contributing member of a team, of a family, or of any type of group is a guiding goal which Adler believes is an essential requirement for the three major problem areas of life—vocation, community living, and marriage. Guiding goals often foster a neurotic style of life such as dominating others, exploiting people, or being exempted from work and responsibilities.

We Live by Fictions. We have noted that one's guiding goal is a major influence in one's style of life; thus the nature of the guiding goal is extremely important. Nevertheless, Adler believed strongly that guiding goals are fictional; that is, they may actually be false interpretations of things. All our ideas of things are our own personal constructions or interpretations. This point is not apparent when we deal with concrete objects such as a tree, a table, or a desk. Personal interpretation becomes more obvious in the case of more abstract or complicated matters such as the meaning of a friend's remarks, the interpretation of beauty, the assignment of value, and so forth.

Our very survival depends on accurate perception and interpretation of reality. One of the symptoms of severe personality disturbance is loss of contact with reality. Yet Adler tells us that something as important as a guiding goal may be fictional. It is necessary to make a distinction between a *useful* fiction and a *harmful* one. It is not always possible to test our beliefs, and it is not necessary to do so. I may believe that a friend would be loyal and helpful in time of need, and derive much benefit from this belief, even though it is false. Ordinarily, we do not test our friends for loyalty. A worker who believes that his boss and his company are personally concerned about his welfare is certainly happier than one who believes that he is like a machine which can be replaced. Workers do not usually socialize with their supervisors, so they never really test their belief. When we occasionally learn that a particular belief is a fiction—that is, when a particular friend proves to be unfaithful—then that belief should be altered to fit reality. Whether the future holds good or bad fortune for us is not known; yet many people actually believe that bad luck will occur for them. It would be much more productive to assume that one is lucky, and that good things will happen. This unsupported belief promotes constructive behavior and positive action. We should make sure that our guiding goal is not harmful for us; and we should adopt an attitude of willingness to change our fictions when they no longer serve us in a positive way. A useful fiction at one time in life may lose its value for us, and it should be replaced by other fictions that support effective living. We cannot test the truth or falseness of many beliefs, but we can determine their value for us.

ABNORMAL TYPES

Adler related abnormality of personality development and functioning to the various aspects of his model of man. Everyone experiences inferiority as he strives to improve himself and his circumstances. The beginner and novice sense their inferiority in comparison with the master or expert, whether it be as a homemaker, a craftsman, a physician, or a garage mechanic. The striving to improve constitutes a healthy superiority striving in such instances. Both the sense of inferiority and the striving to overcome it, when normal, promote constructive behaviors. Personality disorders result from a profound sense of inferiority and exaggerated forms of superiority strivings. The person may develop unhealthy compensations and overcompensations. His guiding goal may be highly unrealistic and selfish. The guiding goal may reflect an irrational drive for power, success, or perfection, as well as for other idealistic goals. The inferiority feelings may be so disruptive that the person is driven to establish some type of superiority over others. The resulting behavior may be highly maladaptive and self-defeating.

The case of the pampered child points up an important aspect of the striving for superiority. Adler frequently stressed that the striving for superiority was a desperate attempt to overcome a sense of inferiority. But it should be borne in mind that being in a superior status brings many benefits. The sickly child enjoys a privileged position in the family. Being the life of the party, or the admired leader, or the most talented member of a crowd satisfies many basic needs, and often these positions are sought for their own sake. We are always seeking to establish the extent of our capabilities and our personal effectiveness. Abnormality occurs when the individual strives in vain to establish his superiority, rather than accepting his position. The desperate striving for superiority may be due to the unwillingness to be simply an average member of a group.

Safeguarding Tendencies and Barricades

In order to create a sense of adequacy, one may use what Adler called safeguarding tendencies. These are protective devices, similar to Freud's defense mechanisms. For example, a common way of dealing with difficult situations is by getting sick. The child may learn early in life that he can be excused from unpleasant tasks by illness, or by the pretense of illness. This may become an habitual pattern of behavior: The person becomes sickly and frail, although there may not be anything really wrong. We are all tempted to find a way out of facing the many problems of growing up and living, but somehow we muster the courage to face them. The sickly person gains a measure of superiority because he is not judged by the same standards which are applied to everyone else. Adler used the term barricades to describe various withdrawal techniques such as shyness, weakness, tiredness, and sensitivity of all sorts. Such devices may preserve the sense of self-esteem by keeping the individual out of the mainstream of life. If the person claims to have a great talent, it is never really put to the test. The undiscovered composer, artist, or writer may nourish a fantasy of greatness for years. Safeguarding tendencies provide an excuse for failure.

Neurosis, A Cowardly Orientation to Life

There are many aspects of neurosis which have been stressed: superficiality of self, childishness, overdeveloped conscience, and repression. But Adler's, perhaps, is the most descriptive. For Adler, the neurotic is a coward; one who avoids facing the requirements of living. The neurotic avoids work and any form of frustration at all cost. He is convinced that his sufferings and hardships are much greater than anyone else's; thus he easily sets himself apart as being something rather special and extraordinary. He has more difficulty with the major tasks of life because his cowardly orientation prevents him from dealing with his problems. He is always looking for exemptions, for an easy way out, yet he craves great success and respect.

An essential aspect of neurosis is the preoccupation with self. The neurotic is a highly selfish person for whom other people are one of the major problems in life. The neurotic is so preoccupied with his own problems that he does not consider other people. In a sense, the neurotic is like a grown-up child. The social sentiments are not highly developed. Just as the coward is very much concerned about his own life, so the neurotic is not sensitive to the needs and feelings of others. He often hurts people without realizing that he is doing so. He is frequently puzzled by the reactions he receives from others because he cannot understand why they are angry, hurt, or slighted. He does not understand because he is so wrapped up in himself that he does not even perceive his own selfish behavior. Adler was insistent that one should learn to be courageous and be willing to tolerate pain and sorrow. Children who are pampered and overprotected are not really prepared for life.

IDEAL PERSONALITY AND LIVING

We can learn about ideal personality and living by looking at what a personality therapist does with his clients or patients. Adler sought to develop a warm and friendly relationship with his patients for the purpose of gaining respect and confidence. His approach was probably the first reality therapy. He encouraged a realistic orientation to life's problems by gently but firmly helping his patients face their unrealistic notions of things and people. The past was probed not to uncover the unconscious but to identify the neurotic style of life. He believed that earliest memories and experiences might reveal this style of living. He urged his patients to begin living on the useful side of life; and above all, he worked to encourage the social tendencies in the patient. In most cases the primary difficulty was lack of real social feeling.

Adler became convinced that man is selfish by nature, but that social tendencies are also a part of man's nature. We need other people to satisfy many of our most basic needs and desires—love, sex, companionship, working partner or team, friends and acquaintances, models. The social aspect is apparently weaker than the more selfish drives; thus social interests should be supported by the important people in the life of the growing child. The mature person does many things as a result of social interests and concerns. Even when he is working for his own ends, it is usually in a social setting and in cooperation with others—family, work setting, member of the community. Adler believed that one should work to improve and perfect himself and to overcome inferiority feelings in social settings. The highest attributes of a person stem from well-developed and social feelings. These feelings temper the power drive and make a person responsive to the needs of others.

Perhaps the concept of the creative self is Adler's most important principle. It is similar to the traditional idea of man as a free agent. It plays an important role in the formation of the style of life; it is the basis for change in personality. There would be no point in personality therapy unless there is a potential for change; and the creative self is the agent that is at work in effective therapy. We can change our own circumstances and reactions by making things happen the way we want them to be. Adler strongly believed that we are not the helpless victims of our unconscious mind, or of our past or present circumstances. Above all, we can even surmount our own selfishness and allow the social side of our nature greater opportunity for expression. We can learn self-control, how to arrange priorities and satisfy our needs, how to work toward goals, and how to express our values in our everyday behavior. Consider the matter of getting something done. We can learn to push ourselves by doing one thing more, or by taking the first step even if it is a small one. The creative self exercises much control over how we perceive things. Many of our problems are a matter of false interpretations of reality which leads us to exaggerate the difficulty of a situation. We may also use the creative self to establish a plan with clearly defined objectives and the proper means of attaining them. The creative self can bring unity and integration within personality. Adler strongly believed that the forces of the creative self should be harnessed as the individual gives up his useless fictions and courageously directs his efforts instead to the areas of life in which he can function effectively.

The Struggle for Security and Self-Awareness: Karen Horney

6

Dr. Karen Horney (1885-1952) was born in Hamburg, Germany, and came to the United States early in the depression of the 1930s. She distinguished herself as a physician and psychiatrist, and was instrumental in pioneering the acceptance of women in medicine. Her experiences in this country gradually led her to see that Freud had not stressed enough the influences of culture. She came to believe that the practices and standards of a society would actually foster abnormalities. In order to grow normally in such a society, a person had to be rather fortunate. Everyone has some of the scars that result from faulty expectations, early harsh experiences, impossible demands at school, vocational uncertainty, and so on. Rather than being the victims of frustrated sex urges, her patients seemed to be more troubled by such concerns as finding suitable work, keeping up with bill payments, and meeting severe competition. Frequently, the greatest difficulty was the loss of contact with the real self, the inability to know who one really is.

Dr. Horney sharply disagreed with the idea that women are inferior to men. She demonstrated by her own example that a woman could follow a professional career and still be a home-maker, if she uses some ingenuity, and is given a chance. She pursued an active career as lecturer, writer, and practicing psychiatrist while bringing up five daughters. She wrote five popular books in the area of personality study.

BASIC CONCEPTS AND PRINCIPLES

Striving for Security

Dr. Horney believed that the basic striving in life is for security. She included, under security, the survival drive. The urge for security is especially strong when a person is faced with basic anxiety. It is perhaps the most painful of human experiences in its intense form. Horney described basic anxiety as the feeling of being utterly helpless and alone in facing a serious problem: The more at stake, the more anxiety there is.

A condition of helplessness is the most conspicuous thing about an infant or a young child, when he does not have functional ways of dealing with his environment and of satisfying his needs. It is obvious that basic anxiety could reach high intensities on occasions, even with the best of care. Strategies to cope with basic anxiety begin to be formed during this time of life, forming the core of a style of life. A key idea in Horney's model is that the style of life may be primarily defensive, a desperate response to basic anxiety. The style of life is formed because it does produce some security, but at the cost of personality distortion and limitation of growth. We may contrast the use of a cave as protection against the elements with the modern luxurious home: Both are means of security, but the modern home fosters the good life much more than the rigors of the cave.

Three Relationships to People

Moving Toward People. A rather passive child who has
dominant parents may develop a social orientation of moving
toward people. An outstanding characteristic of this type of
orientation is the striving to be liked or loved by those who are
important to the individual. Being loved by those who have
control of your life means that they will bestow favors. All that
one has to do is to submit, to cooperate, to hold back on strong
personal feelings, and in general, to be compliant. This compliant
life style certainly suits many people; and we would have to agree
with Dr. Horney that it does help one to gain security. If you are
successful in being liked or loved, you certainly have a valuable
asset, and you can get far if you use this ability well. But Dr.
Horney notes that this orientation can be neurotic because it works
in its extreme form to stunt personality. To always be nice, loving,
and cooperative surely requires that one hold back and repress
some of his most important needs. Certainly we cannot get along
with others if we always seek to get our own way, or to set
standards for others; but undeviating cooperation and submission
are also injurious to our own personal development and functioning. In the end, we may lose the respect of others if we display an
inability to assert our own rights and demands.

Moving Against People.   Some children discover that they can
get their way with their parents, and with people in general, by
being forceful and fighting for what they want. Again, the natures
of both the child and his parents are important in the development
of this type of social approach. One may find that other people
usually submit to him if he pushes hard for what he wants. The
outstanding characteristic of this life style is using people as a
means of getting what one wants. If you have the ability to get
your point across and elicit cooperation from others, you can
certainly use this to your advantage. But like the compliant
person, the power-driven person has to sacrifice things, particularly if he is compulsively driven to be superior and dominant in
his social relationships. Security is certainly promoted by this

orientation, but again, at the cost of not satisfying some basic needs. The person who is motivated to exploit others cannot allow his more human emotions to be expressed: He cannot allow the luxury of simply being himself because he is always driven to dominate and win. He may appreciate that others do not really like him, but he cannot do anything to hold back his desire to dominate. Of course, we are talking about the more extreme cases, which Horney believed result in neurotic behavior.

Moving Away from People. Some children find the best way to deal with their parents is to stay away from them. Parents' inconsistent behavior toward their children may promote a detached orientation to life. The outstanding characteristic of this life style is the avoidance of problems associated with social relationships. A person may have difficulty obtaining love from others and getting his own way, so he avoids both alternatives by isolation. His ideal in life is to be self-sufficient, so that he does not need other people. He limits his social activities. There is no question that relating to people causes many problems; and for some, the most difficult problems in living center around social relationships. So why not avoid such problems by being a loner? The answer is rather obvious: For the sake of avoiding anxiety, a person makes a needless sacrifice.

The Three Orientations to Living and Decision-Making

The styles of life—social contacts, power and domination over others, or detachment and self-sufficiency—have much to do with satisfying basic needs and making important decisions about life. Should we seek the love and approval of others or dominate them and use them for our selfish purposes? Should we seek to master as many situations as possible, or to be easygoing and carefree about life? Should we work hard to achieve or is it better to enjoy a rich private life? Although the answers are not clearly one way or the other, much does depend on how we answer them; and of course we may have already taken a stand, although we do not realize it.

Glamorous Roles for the Three Orientations

Who tells the growing child what to do and be? Important adults set the standards, and these are usually presented in a highly glamorous and attractive manner. Each of the three orientations which Horney proposes has a number of heroes. With respect to the orientation of moving toward people: who does not admire the true lover of mankind, the humane and considerate person who would do almost anything for a friend? With respect to the orientation of manipulating people: who would not want to be the conquering hero, the masterful person who knows how to come out on top of everything? Finally, regarding the self-sufficient orientation: these are idealized in the mystic, the rugged individualistic American farmer, or the sage and scholar, all who are supposedly above worldly things. Certainly a young person would rather select the ideal, the glamorous, and the spectacular than the average and ordinary. By striving for such unattainable goals, abnormal behaviors are quite likely to develop. For example, one may begin to think of himself as having the attributes of one of the cultural models, and gradually the life style of that model is considered to be one's own real self. This distortion of the real self is, according to Horney, the beginning of a neurotic process in which the person eventually loses contact with his real self; he becomes artificial and phony. The consequences are quite serious. We all suffer from this process to some degree.

ABNORMAL TYPES

Neurosis

Dr. Horney was greatly concerned with neurosis, and wrote her first book on it: *The Neurotic Personality Of Our Time.* She believed that everyone has both constructive and destructive forces in his personality, but that in a neurotic, the destructive forces predominate. Her idea of neurosis centered about two processes: *neurotic needs and neurotic conflicts.*

Neurotic Needs

Horney held that a need is neurotic if it meets four characteristics: (1) if it is compulsive; (2) if it is exaggerated; (3) if it is extremely general; and (4) if it is never satisfiable.

A need is compulsive when a person feels driven to satisfy it. There is no compromise possible. "I must have a college degree, or life will be utterly empty and not worth living. If I do not have a beautiful home, I cannot possibly be happy." Often, the goal is highly glamorous and idealistic. The person may be seeking perfection, and of course, he is bound to be frustrated. The compulsive nature of the need will not allow any moderation, and the person continues to strive for the unattainable despite repeated frustrations. He may become extremely bitter and critical of other people whom he imagines are the cause of his failure. By contrast, the normal person moderates his needs if it becomes clear that he cannot satisfy them to the extent that his original ambitions demanded. He postpones and compromises, and even turns to substitutes.

The satisfaction of a certain need—such as for love, power, or self-sufficiency—may be the only way a person has to gain security for himself, so he may go to extremes with it. He may never get enough love, or power, or self-sufficiency, depending on which one is dominant. The actions taken to satisfy the dominant need may be so extreme that they involve practically everything a person does. To be loved and to impress everyone is the ideal of the person who moves toward others. For one who moves against people, every social contact is a win or lose situation. The detached person may strive for total freedom of obligation: He does not want to be indebted to others in any way.

Finally, when does the insecure person get enough love, or power, or self-sufficiency? Partial satisfaction may only intensify the desires and the desperate pursuit. A condition of instability develops, until even when the person has what ordinarily would be considered satisfactory, it is still not enough.

Neurotic Conflicts

Horney was especially concerned with two types of inner conflicts: the conflict between the real self and the ideal self, and the conflicts among the three basic orientations to living—moving toward people, away from people, and against people. Conflict means that there is opposition, that certain components are competing. Frustration, tension, and unrest inevitably result. The person is torn by the warring factions, and cannot find peace of mind. Furthermore, one cannot use his abilities effectively when he is being torn apart by his inner conflicts. One of the most tragic aspects of neurosis is that while the person strives for perfection and the best of life, he is crippled by his own neurotic needs and inner conflicts. Using his abilities inefficiently and even in self-defeating ways, he ends up as a failure in meeting his most basic needs.

The Real Self Versus the Ideal Self.   The basic inner conflict takes place between what we really are and what we think we are. We may believe that we are popular and likeable, but we may actually be just the opposite. In this instance, we have the very real problem of dealing with the painful evidence, however, because we cannot avoid situations in which the real facts are quite obvious. The only way we can preserve our good opinion of self is to deny, distort, or disguise information; this is a highly irrational approach to reality.

People treat us inconsistently: Some like us and some treat us as if we were uninteresting and unlikeable. One attempts to form a concept or image of one's self from this conflicting information; and, like any other concept or image, it may be more or less correct. We have already noted that glamorous roles are portrayed to the growing person, so that one may simply begin to take one of these as his image of self. In other words, the person may have a highly glamorized but totally wrong image of self. Of course, we act upon this image; we try to fulfill the expectations that are associated with it. But the attributes of the real self are continually confusing the picture. Rather than changing the image, some people contrive certain neurotic distortions—such as converting their needs to claims and making over their personality by shoulds. Their image of self is supported by unrealistic expectations both external to themselves and of themselves.

A need becomes a claim when the person converts a desire into a demand. "I want people to like me" is converted into "I have a right" or "I deserve to be liked by everyone." "It is unfair when I am not liked." The claim is a way of adding a personal due to the need. A person justifies his claim on the basis of being good, being sincere, or liking people. If the claim is frustrated, the person feels that he has been dealt with unjustly because after all, it was something that he deserved. We get hurt by other people, and of course, no one enjoys that; but one who has a claim that others should always be sensitive to his feelings is especially hurt because he believes that it is a violation of a right. This point explains the extreme reaction we often observe in some people when they are slighted or blocked in any way. They seem to say that they are very special, and that this should not have happened to them. Making claims is a neurotic way of molding the world according to one's image. Claims can take many forms—not being criticized, doubted, or questioned; being entitled to immunity and exception; receiving claims of honor from everyone; and claiming not to have any problems.

A perfect person not only demands a good environment, but, he must also, of course, have the necessary desirable attributes. Rather than working for these, the person who has developed an idealized notion of self simply begins to believe and act as though he already possessed the favorable attributes. They exist as inner dictates, or "shoulds." "Shoulds" are perfectionistic expectations of self such as being always calm and composed in social settings, having just the right comeback in an interchange with a rival, being able to make good grades without much effort, being on top of every situation, and so on. Sometimes the expectations are conflicting, as when one expects to be both loving and dominating in social relationships. The shoulds stem from a false pride: The person really thinks too much of himself. An interesting contradiction occurs in one who has many shoulds: There is both too much self-love and too much self-hate. The person may behave at one time as if he were the greatest human alive, and at another time as if he were the most despicable and unworthy person who ever lived. Horney explained this apparent contradiction in the conflict between the real self and the ideal self. We cannot help noting our real attributes and accomplishments from time to time, thus our glorious image of self is brought under question, and there is self-hatred. But when the ideal self reigns, then there is neurotic pride, an inordinate self love.

It might be interesting to compare Horney's notion of the neurotic with two others, Freud's and Adler's. Freud seemed to say that the neurotic was childish—self-centered, immature, pleasure-seeking. Adler found the neurotic to be a coward—always trying to get away with things, looking for the easy way out, wanting a privileged status. Horney's neurotic is a phony—artificial, pretentious, play acting. He puts on a real display for the sake of making a hit. He pretends so frequently that he begins to believe his own lies. Claims and shoulds contribute to the artificial glamour of the ideal self.

Conflicts Among the Three Basic Styles of Life

The other sources of inner conflict are the three major directions of living. The person who always seeks the love of others must practically obliterate his self because he tries to make himself attractive to others. He contorts his personality to fit the model of a compliant, loving, and cooperative person; but he gives up many of his most personal desires, and never really feels like a whole person.

The person who always strives for power over others is so busy fighting to get his way that he has to deny or distort some of his most basic desires. When someone does him an injustice, there is no question as to the course of action: He fights and complains, and takes whatever steps he can to get even or to win out. But such a rigid approach is not always the best course. He is also troubled by his lack of human warmth, and by his inability to be independent of others. His orientation also requires people, even if only to use them. This is a weakness which causes conflict: that is, the conflict between getting what he wants through people and being self-sufficient and masterful without them.

The detached orientation leads to the conflict between doing things alone and working with others. A person cannot do everything alone, and so he is forced into situations of dependence. Furthermore, there is the matter of vital needs that involve other people—love, sex, companionship, and friendship. These needs cannot simply be denied without experiencing frustration. The conflicts are the result of these opposing needs.

IDEAL PERSONALITY AND LIVING

Horney was a practicing psychiatrist who was primarily concerned with getting rid of symptoms. Her work was not with normal people, but we can certainly draw from her model. One thing is clear: We can guard against the factors that make for neurosis. We should keep a close check on our concept of self by observing our behavior in a variety of situations. We may believe that we are balanced and objective about things; but if we observe our own behavior, it may turn out that we have a rather glamorous concept of ourselves, and that we expect a great deal from others. By observing the things that are especially frustrating for us, we may become acquainted with the needs that have been converted to claims. Furthermore, our self expectations, our shoulds, may be appropriate to a superhuman. We can also become aware of the dominant direction of our behavior: Do we work primarily for love and approval, for power and domination, or to be independent of others? The ideal is to do all three flexibly, according to the situation: One should be willing to submit at times, to fight and assert the self at others, and to be self-sufficient when necessary.

Self-Awareness and Self-Exploration

Horney gives us a simple formula for liberating the forces of the real self and setting the conditions for actualizing these potentialities: self-awareness. We ought to work at becoming acquainted with our true self and its components. In her book on self-analysis she compares the self to the complexities of a large city. If one wished to know how the city is run he would visit the governing agencies—the city hall, the court house, the welfare agency, and so on. In the same way, we should become acquainted with our own governing forces—our needs and goals, our claims and shoulds, our aspirations for the future, and our basic assumptions about ourselves. We should certainly try to experience our real feelings and emotions, for these are often the very things that get distorted and squelched. Our ideal image of self may totally cut us off from our feelings and emotions, so that we are not even sure of what we feel about things.

Living Is Therapeutic

Is it necessary to undergo psychiatric treatment to live effectively? Horney certainly advises such treatment for those who simply cannot help themselves; but she believed that this is not the case with most people. Living can be therapeutic, if one takes the proper attitude. A person who is open to new experiences can learn from both the positive and negative things that occur in his life. We learn by observing others, by fitting together the things that are happening to us, by becoming aware of our skills, by profiting from past mistakes, and in a great variety of ways. Even people who reach advanced age tell us that they are still learning the art of living. We certainly can learn from our friends. In many ways a friend is like a psychiatrist because he can help us to understand ourselves by discussing things with us. A friend can help us express emotions that may get all blocked up inside. Above all, there is mutual sharing and support: We may come to see that our problems are not unique, and that everyone is struggling with similar life problems. Horney was quite optimistic about our possibilities for effective living, and she felt that everyone could harness the constructive growth forces that are present in all of us.

HUMANISTIC-EXISTENTIAL MODELS: SELF-CONSCIOUS AND FUTURE-ORIENTED MAN

III

If you were going to put together a model which represents man, you would have the challenging and difficult task of determining what components to include in your model, and how much weight to give each of them. Would you stress biological drives and selfish concerns? How much weight would you give to negative emotions such as hatred, envy, jealousy, and the killer instinct? What would full development and ideal functioning be, and what environmental conditions would be required to promote these ideals? What place would you give to inborn tendencies, and how much stress would you assign to learning potential? Humanistic psychologists have included in their models of man the notion of the self or ego as a free agent. They hold that a person can control his own destiny if conditions are not too restrictive. They also see man as having the ability for self-examination or self-reflection. We can rationally interpret, criticize, and evaluate our own behavior, both present and past. We also have the ability, according to the humanistic psychologists, to plan for the future and to anticipate the long-term consequences of present behavior. Many people do not actually function on these distinctively human levels, but the fact that they can provides a great challenge for behavioral scientists and other leaders of the community. Take away any of the ingredients which the humanistic psychologists have included in their models of man, and the result is something less than a human being. The humanistic and existential models portray man as having much greater potential for satisfying living than do other models. Anything less than their ideals for man is considered abnormal. Failure to promote the positive human attributes is the cause of personality disturbances and destructive and criminal behavior.

Given the distinctively human attributes mentioned above, certain problems and tasks naturally follow. In other words, because man is made the way he is, he must face certain problems; and it turns out that some of these simply cannot be solved. We all have conflicts that we cannot completely eliminate. Being human presents us with existential problems, that is, problems of living, such as facing an unknown future, having to make decisions with only partial information, and living with the discrepancy between what is and what should be. As a conscious and self-conscious, future-oriented, creative, reasoning personality, we must cope with certain problems created by these very qualities.

Maturity and the Developing Self: Gordon W. Allport

7

Not long ago, the young science of psychology was struggling to find and establish its identity. Because human nature is so complex, it is possible to take a variety of approaches to it. Should we begin with what goes on in personal experience, or should we observe what can be seen and measured? Should we attempt to learn about human nature in general—about what is common to all people—or should we focus on concepts and principles that could help us understand the individual? Should we look to the past or to the future in a person's life? Should we stress conscious or unconscious factors? Should we include the study of animal behavior as a means of getting to know about man? These issues threatened to destroy the young science of psychology, but it was pioneers such as the late Gordon W. Allport who helped to point the way that psychology should follow.

Allport (1897-1967) was daring enough to take an unpopular stand in psychology. He pioneered in the area of the scientific study of the individual. He felt that we needed a science that could tell us how to know the single individual. Disagreeing with other psychologists, he did not believe that the mature human was a grown-up child, a more complex animal, a complicated machine, or an "insane" person that had been civilized. Moreover, he held that the mature person is not driven by unconscious forces over which he has no control. He believed that the mature person knows pretty much what he wants and where he is going. His study was focused on the unique individual: the highly complex, mature adult. Although the accepted approach in psychology was to study concepts and principles that would help to understand mankind, Allport felt that we should know how to study the particular person, ourselves included, in order to ultimately improve the conditions of life for all of us. He wanted to direct attention to the unique complex of qualities that made up the mature adult, his ideal for personality growth and functioning.

Allport believed that some of the early psychologists had created a distorted view of man. Freud, for instance, worked with seriously disturbed neurotics. He was a practicing psychoanalyst and the founder of that school of psychology. He was fully concerned with treating psychologically disordered patients who had tried all else and in desperation came to him for help. He built a model of man that was appropriate for the neurotic personality: one who is driven by unknown forces, one who has had past hurtful though unconscious experiences, one who has never learned to live comfortably with his basic drives, or one who has not been able to relate to other people in a satisfactory manner. What he learned about the distorted personalities he applied to everyone; and he came to believe that the normal was simply a moderate form of the same picture: that normal and abnormal are matters of degree. Allport felt that this view was totally distorted. He began the movement of studying normal, and even the most highly developed, humans. His study led him to the conclusion that the properly developed and fully functioning human required a model that was totally different from the one that Freud had formulated.

We will treat Allport's model of personality from the standpoint of its growth and development and the characteristics of the mature personality. In highlighting the differences between the mature and immature adult and the child we will consider the following topics: growth of the knowing functions; growth of motivation; the nature of goal striving; adult intentions; and the growth of self. Allport was especially concerned with expanding self-experiences as the person grows. He delineated seven distinct aspects of the self that emerge at different times during the growth of the individual. He maintained maturity depended upon the proper development of all the aspects of self: 1) bodily self, 2) self-identity, 3) self-esteem, 4) self-image, 5) self-extension, 6) self as a problem solver and 7) the sense of striving for goals. Allport pinpointed the attributes of the mature personality by specifying eight key requirements: self-extension; warm social relationships; emotional security; realistic perception; useful skills; worthwhile assignments; being objective about self and guiding purpose, goals, values. In fitting together the various elements of Allport's model, the reader should keep in mind the major objective, the attributes of the fully developed and mature adult.

BASIC CONCEPTS AND PRINCIPLES

Child Versus Adult

What happens to us as we grow up? Is everyone basically a child underneath it all? Do we really have the same motives and conflicts throughout life? Some psychologists, such as Freud, believe that the child can be found in all of us, no matter how mature we appear. But Allport believed that Freud is right only in the case of those who are abnormal. Like Freud, he believed that the abnormal person has many childish carry-overs, many unresolved early conflicts that continue to become activated, many irrational protective strategies from his past. Allport traced the development of the faculties of a normal person—knowing and understanding drives and motives, the development of the self, the changes in social encounters—and he saw not only greater complexity in personality, but many new dimensions that the child does not have. The mature person has a totally different orientation to life and to himself than the immature person or neurotic.

Growth of the Knowing Functions

As the child grows up, the remarkable thing is that he begins more and more to know his world. The normal adult has the ability to imagine things, to form concepts, to fit pieces together mentally, and in general, to think about the things going on all about him and within him. The child is primarily a reactor, now responding to this external stimulus and now to that. He finds his drives difficult to manage because his knowing functions are immature.

Allport gives us a general model of the developing individual from dependence to independence to responsibility. At first we are totally dependent on the environment; gradually we acquire knowledge and skills and become more and more independent of it. With maturity we again relate to our environment in a dependent way; but then, under the control of guiding ideals, we become responsible through our own choices.

Knowledge helps us to control our automatic responses and impulses. We reason out a course of action rather than responding directly to a stimulus. Allport did not accept the idea that man is like a robot which is governed by learned habits and instinctive behaviors. When the child learns language, the mental apparatus takes on a very different character. We talk to ourselves about our circumstances. We tell ourselves things that make those circumstances worse, or, perhaps, better than they are. We are strongly motivated to know things as accurately as possible. When something happens, our mental powers immediately go to work to analyze, synthesize, compare and contrast, and recall past experiences until we work out a course of action. Man is not a bundle of habits; he is characterized more by his ability to know and choose. In fact, we can judge one's maturity on the basis of to what extent his responses are either impulsive and habitual or the product of thinking and reasoning. We are capable of knowing, of forming insights, of constructing a plan of action, and of working things out mentally before carrying them out. The knowing and reasoning powers are absent in the infant, and immature in the child; but they should be fully developed in adulthood as we attain independent status. If this development does not occur, the person becomes abnormal.

Growth of Motivation

Could it be possible that the same drives and motives are active throughout life? Some psychologists think so. They believe that we have the same drives, urges, and impulses, but that we find different outlets for them. The adult and the child may not like the same food, but the hunger drive is present throughout life. The need for attention seems to emerge early in life. The child will make noise, interrupt his parents, and even break things in order to get attention. Although differently expressed, the need for attention also seems to persist throughout life. This view holds that we may learn how to cover up a bit and not let our motives be so obvious, but that basically, we still want and need what the child does.

Allport disagreed strongly with this view. He believed that this description of motivation is a good characterization of the stunted, the neurotic, and the disordered personality; but that it is totally wrong when applied to the mature, fully developed personality. Obviously, the adult—mature or otherwise—has the same basic drives as the child. The organismic drives are with us from the cradle to the grave. But even such drives occupy a very different place in the life of the child and that of the mature adult. Often a child does not know what to do with his drives, but the mature person puts them in their place. He takes care of them adequately without too much preoccupation, and goes on to other things. It is the immature and the underdeveloped personality that equates drive satisfaction with happiness; thus, even in the case of basic drives, we see a striking difference in the manner in which they are gratified and the place they occupy in one's life.

Concern with Goals Rather Than Drives.   The mature person works out short-term and long-term goals. The highest achievements of man are associated with goals rather than drives. Drive reduction leads to relaxation and inactivity; achieving goals stimulates activity. Drives produce tension and so do goals; but the tension of drives is much stronger than that of goals. Thus, many people concentrate exclusively on taking care of their drives. They cannot work very hard or very long on desirable long-term goals. The mature person works out methods of making his long-term goals important enough to sustain effort in getting them accomplished. There are techniques which can increase the tensions associated with goal-attainment so that they compete more favorably with the more powerful drives. Thus the needs for relaxation, for excitement, for socializing, and other powerful motives can be successfully resisted so that certain unpleasant tasks or necessary behaviors can get under way. If you think about the matter briefly, it should be quite clear that the most important things in your life are related to long-term goals rather than to immediate drives or needs. You can judge the maturity of a person by the manner in which he works toward his long-term objectives.

Intentions, the Major Adult Motives.   Allport proposed that the motivations of the mature adult are best characterized as intentions. An intention brings together both knowledge and striving. As one comes to know the value of a particular goal, the desire for it increases. Allport made an interesting point about getting to know ourselves and others. It is not enough to have a knowledge of needs, because not every need will be satisfied. It is not enough to know what abilities a person has because, again, not all abilities may be perfected and used. It is not even enough to know certain personality traits, because one may deliberately work toward an objective even when he does not have the most desirable personal attributes. All these things are important, but the best single thing to know is a person's intentions. One's intentions may override needs, such as postponing the desire to marry for the sake of finishing college; one's intentions may direct abilities, as when a gifted performer gives up a music career for the sake of teaching; and intentions may turn a shy and timid person into a decisive and aggressive leader under certain conditions. For example, President Truman, who was mild mannered and shy, had to make some of the most difficult decisions presented to a president of the U.S. His intention to protect his country provided the motive force for such difficult decisions as dropping the first atomic bomb over Japan. It is clear that intentions bring into focus the future and frequently involve the enduring frustration of immediate needs; thus some people's motivation is primarily the result of needs rather than intentions. Maturity can be judged in terms of the extent to which a person is motivated by personally determined intentions.

How Does Motivation Change?   One of the most fundamental questions we can ask about any behavior is the motivation behind it. Freud made a great contribution to psychology by showing that much of human motivation was irrational, selfish, and drive-related. Freud was always looking for the irrational, the primitive, the sexual, the unconscious in his patients. But again, we should bear in mind that he was dealing with the motivation of sick personalities. Allport studied the mature personality and found a very different picture of motivation. While Freud seemed to reduce everything to frustrated drives, Allport held that we do many things because we like to do them, and for no other reason. At first, a man works to satisfy his basic survival needs; but later he often finds his job activities satisfying in their own right. He may continue working after retirement age because he enjoys his work. This picture may be somewhat incomplete unless we take into account the fact that several motives are usually satisfied by the same activity. A job earns a salary, which causes pride in oneself; working with others satisfies the need for companionship, and perhaps the need for competition as well. But surely an important part of the motivational picture is the work activity itself. We could go on, as Allport did, to relate one's work to the image of self, to fulfillment of personally developed intentions; but the important thing is that much of what we do has no basic motivation except the doing itself. In other words, we do many things simply because we like and enjoy doing them, and among these things are included some of man's noblest activities. A father may take on a second job for the sake of sending his son or daughter to college. A woman may volunteer many hours helping sick patients because she is convinced that the work is important. There are many instances when a particular behavior is the outcome of frustrated basic needs, such as showing off, competing with father for mother's approval, overcoming inferiority. These are examples of the type of motivation which Freud found in his patients, but Allport found the motivation of mature people to be independent of basic needs.

Allport believed that no aspect of the developing personality is as essential for healthy growth and functioning as the self. He related maturity and immaturity to the growth of the self. The full development of the self is a protracted process, and any defect in the evolving self may permanently block the fulfillment of one's potentialities. The reader might examine his own self-experiences according to the analysis which Allport delineated in order to gain an appreciation of this most important aspect of personality.

Growth of the Self

Allport has done a great deal with the study of the self, a most difficult topic for experimental psychologists. Many psychologists have even denied that there is such a thing as the self, but Allport undertook a thorough analysis of the various ways we experience ourselves. What a difference it makes, Allport believed, when we do something with self-involvement rather than without it. Switch on the self and what you learn, feel, and do takes on a completely different significance. You can read something passively many times and you will retain very little of it unless you want to learn the material. There once was a schoolmaster who read a morning prayer at chapel every day for twenty years; but one day the prayer book was missing and he floundered and sputtered the prayer incorrectly. Working at something which is routine, uninteresting, or simply required, usually involves the lowest levels of motivation; but once one becomes self-involved, everything is sparked up.

Allport asked the interesting question: How is the self experienced as it grows? He held that the self-experiences broaden in complexity as the self grows. With this growth, the self is not just felt as an "I", or as an agent that receives and acts upon things.

Bodily Self. I feel myself as a body of certain dimensions. The sense of body is probably the least important sense of self, ordinarily, but it can be a problem. Many people have an unhealthy body image. They feel abnormal in size, shape, or in texture of skin, and so on. A healthy sense of bodily self is essential for adequate development of the personality.

Self-Identity. Identity is experienced gradually and is composed of the most personal, or most central, defining traits. It is most nearly the "I" in the sense of a continuing core self. A well-established sense of identity makes for stability in personality; and any disturbance in identity affects all aspects of personality growth and functioning. Allport agreed with Erikson, who developed the idea of the identity crisis as the most critical problem in becoming an adult.

Self-Esteem. One of our most important self-experiences is liking or disliking the self. When Allport spoke of self-esteem, he meant something like pride or self-respect. At first the source of pride is external, and if development is normal, it becomes a matter of personal evaluation. The child responds to praise and punishment, to love and disapproval, with corresponding changes in self-esteem. We can never completely remove our self-esteem from the opinions of others; but in normal development the valuation of self is more personal. If one lives up to a self-image which is of his own making, then he feels pride; if not, he feels a sense of unworthiness. The self-image we refer to is another aspect of the developing self; and of course, any distortion in that aspect will create problems in self-worth. A normal person has a good sense of self-worth; he does respect and like himself, but not in the sense of being conceited, haughty, proud, or feeling superior to others.

Self-Image. Allport pointed out that we experience ourselves in the form of an image, or concept. We have a natural tendency to understand things by forming an image or concept of them. So we may form an image of ourselves as helpless and weak, strong and capable, or unlovable; or as a liberated woman, or a suave and charming gentleman. Just as we tend to form a single image or concept to depict another person, we do the same for ourselves. Obviously, our image or concept of others and of ourselves may be essentially correct, or it may be distorted in varying degrees. Many problems may develop when our self-image is distorted.

Another aspect of the self-image is the formation of images of possible selves. As the person develops, he begins to appreciate the difference between what he thinks he is and what he should be, or could be, or what others wants him to be. These images of possible selves are extremely important in determining future striving, and have much to do with growing fully and becoming a mature person.

Self-Extension.   I can experience myself as liking or loving things. The extended self means what is important and valued by the self. In an important way, what a person loves is an extension of that person. Allport believed that self-extensions are absolutely necessary for living the good life. A normal person needs to be personally involved in at least some aspects of life. Lacking self-extension not only leads to an empty and routine life, but also, in the case of preoccupation with oneself, produces many personality problems.

Self as a Problem Solver.   The self is beginning to attain its full adult status when the person begins to sense and use his abilities to reason and to solve problems. The feeling that the self is competent to do things is essential for maturity. To be good in some things is one of the ingredients of growing up normally. A profound sense of inferiority may result from a distortion of this aspect of self.

The Sense of Striving for Goals.   Probably the most outstanding aspect of the mature self is the sense of striving toward long-term goals. The self is fully developed when the person can look at himself and his accomplishments and set goals for the future. We have already indicated that Allport felt that goal-setting and goal-striving are the major defining qualities of the mature person.

Growth of Conscience

An important aspect of the developing self is conscience. Allport distinguished between the "must" conscience of the child and the "ought" conscience of the mature adult. The difference is quite significant. A child does many things because he "must" do them—because someone who could punish him forced him to do them. His own conscience then takes over and issues strict orders. If the self develops properly, there is a change in the nature of conscience. The person does things because he ought to do them, rather than because he must do them. He wishes to fulfill his self-image, his sense of pride, his long-term goals, and his sense of identity. Thus, the "ought" conscience stems from the fully developed self. What a difference in motivation—on the one hand, doing something because of fear, and on the other, doing something because it will help one to become the person one wants to be some day.

An adult may continue experiencing the "must" conscience and do things out of fear: For example, one may continue to practice his childhood religion out of a vague fear or sense of guilt. A child may be forced to ("must") attend the church of his parents; but when he reaches adult status, church attendance should become a matter of "ought" rather than of fear. The mature adult has many things to do that are neither "musts" nor "oughts," but he does them because of the perceived consequences. If I do not empty the rubbish, or change the oil in my car, or pay my bills, some very undesirable consequences may occur. Again, we can judge the degree of maturity in terms of the extent to which the person is governed by "musts" or "oughts," and by reasoned decisions.

Makeup of Personality

Using Allport's model to help us understand the fully developed and mature personality requires that we see the complexity of personality, which Allport brilliantly portrayed. His trait approach displays the many and varied facets of personality and it can help us to fit our observations into a coherent pattern. Allport found that the immature person has many splits and independent sub-personalities which cause conflict and inconsistent behaviors, while the mature person has a self-image which holds together and is supported by the central traits. The major intentions, which constitute the core of the self, exert an organizing influence over the cardinal and central traits.

Cardinal Traits.   Allport's approach to personality study has often been termed "trait psychology." He held that the best way to describe personality is to specify individual traits. A particular trait may be the most outstanding thing about a person, the one which is most conspicuous and which becomes the identifying attribute of that person. He named such traits "cardinal traits." We might say something like: John is a really *ambitious* executive; Mary is a *loving* person; Jack is usually *self-centered.* The italicized words point to cardinal traits.

Central Traits.   While not as all-encompassing as a cardinal trait, certain traits that define the self are called "central traits" by Allport. These traits are most characteristic of a person. They are easily activated; they almost always play a part in what the person is doing; and any change in one of them will be easily sensed as a change in the total personality. Allport has estimated that there are between five and ten of these in the typical person; and if we know all the various aspects of these central traits and their interactions, we have a pretty good picture of the personality. We attempt to express the core of central traits by such descriptive terms as witty, generous, stingy, selfish, spiteful, motherly, radical, conservative, and so forth. We literally have thousands of such descriptive terms, which is an indication of the variety of possible ways in which people differ.

Secondary Traits.   Allport called traits that are rather specific, but which are only occasionally active in the personality, "secondary traits." Mary is nervous when her cousin John comes over. Mary prefers tea to coffee. She likes football more than baseball. These are rather specific, limited traits, which do not reveal further aspects of the person. In fact, these traits could change without changing the essential personality. In getting to know ourselves and others, we should look for the cardinal trait and a handful of central traits. Following Allport's analysis, the task does not seem difficult. It appears that all we have to do is to observe a person, or ourselves, in a variety of circumstances until we get to know the cardinal and central traits. But there is much more to the picture, as Allport saw it, because traits are quite complex.

A trait is activated by certain situations and expressed by certain behaviors. To describe a woman as motherly is only to give a highly general characterization. We would want to know in what situations this trait becomes active and how the trait is expressed. For example, a crying infant, a sick animal, or a feeble old person might activate the motherly trait in a person. As a result, she might feed the infant, nurse the sick animal, or comfort the feeble old person. These behaviors are expressions of the motherly trait. One more point is relevant: There is interaction among all her traits. Motherliness will interact with introversion or extroversion, intelligence, self-centeredness, and all her other central traits. The task of getting to know personality, in Allport's view, is huge. We not only must identify the various core tendencies of traits, but the situations which activate them and the behaviors which express them. We must also learn the various interactions of traits—a very tall order indeed.

ABNORMAL TYPES

We have already examined some of Allport's ideas on abnormalities, and we will consider them more specifically here. Following Allport's model, we can think of abnormality in terms of faulty development of the bodily self, self-identity, self-extensions, self-image, self-esteem, self as a problem-solver, and the self working toward goals. Another form of abnormality can be found in the continuation of the "must" conscience into adulthood, rather than its being replaced by the "ought" conscience. One type of abnormality in which Allport was especially interested was what he called "opportunistic living," by which he meant the preoccupation with drive satisfaction and momentary pleasures. Sick people are preoccupied with their basic drives. The healthy adult is more concerned with the possibilities of his future than the limitations of his past; he is more concerned with long-term goals than with the tension relief of basic drives; and he is more concerned with active participation in life rather than safety and security.

Comparison of Neurotic and Normal

Allport offers several interesting comparisons between the neurotic orientation and the normal orientation to life. We might consider these to get a better picture of both.

1. The neurotic attempts to quickly avoid or escape anything that produces pain or tension, whereas the normal person generally confronts the requirements of his circumstances, and works aggressively to satisfy his needs.

2. The neurotic habitually tries to deny his difficulties; but he usually fails because his problems continue to confront him, often with greater force. The normal person can effectively dispose of certain matters, and not think about them. Thus, just as one might put the unsightly rubbish in the yard instead of the living room, so one might put aside thoughts of death or the unknown future, and get on with tasks that can be accomplished. The normal person distinguishes clearly between problems he can or cannot solve.

3. The neurotic is characterized by many splits in personality; the various parts are not working together. Goals and values may conflict, and opposite trends and traits compete with each other. The normal person is characterized by integration and unity. The various components of his personality support each other. He does not fight himself in getting things done.

4. The neurotic not only tries to deceive others about his true nature; he is actually self-deceiving. He may be unclear about his own motives. The normal person has insight into his motivations and behavior, and is aware of his status and possibilities.

5. The neurotic is characterized by a stunting in personality growth. His emotions may have a primitive quality, and his motives may be childish. The normal person thinks, feels, and acts in accordance with his age expectancies.

6. The neurotic finds his impulses troublesome; he finds himself doing things that he does not understand. The normal person can restrain impulsive expression and tolerate frustration while he works out a course of action: When what he wants is not available to him, he can accept substitutes or nothing at all when no outlet is possible.

7. The neurotic's involvements are narrow and tied to the immediate situation. He may focus all his attention on the one bad experience of the day and forget all the good things that happened. The normal person can remove himself from the immediate situation and survey and evaluate things. In most situations, he can take charge of his own thoughts, feelings, and reactions.

IDEAL PERSONALITY AND LIVING

Now we come to Allport's ideal for personality and living. The reader should bear in mind that the attributes of maturity which we will discuss presuppose the developmental changes in the aspects of personality that we have noted. The developed personality is characterized by a well-formed core of self which includes an "ought" conscience and a system of intentions. The knowing functions operate vigorously and come between the environment and adaptive behavior. The person must work out a value orientation to life, so that there is an order of priority. Allport is very clear in stressing the generality of his model. Each person must apply the attributes in his own individual way. Furthermore, the ideal life is not a static state which is achieved once and for always. Each period of life brings new changes in ourselves and in our circumstances. A mature orientation requires constant adjustment and flexibility.

Self-Extension

Self-extension means to participate in a personal way in some phases of living. Allport held that one cannot be mature unless he is doing something which counts with his self—doing what one considers worthwhile and interesting, at least some of the time. Our faculties are set for action, and their use gives a certain amount of pleasure. Thus simply being absorbed in a task is beneficial to mental health; but if what we are doing involves ourselves we cannot but derive certain pleasures. Our self-extensions may be few and may not be glamorous; but without personal participation in something, life is meaningless.

Warm Social Relationships

Social warmth, as in a close friendship or harmonious marriage, adds a certain zest to life. In order to relate comfortably with others we need to develop the capacity for intimacy and compassion. Intimacy involves many social skills—respecting the other person as he is, accepting his right to hold strong opinions and convictions even if they are different from one's own, and being involved in mutual sharing. The strongest ego extensions can be human attachments. The variety of social contacts is very large, ranging from casual contacts at school or work to family ties, buddy or pal relationships with members of the same sex, and to a deep and abiding intimate love relationship in or out of marriage. Compassion stems from the awareness of the human situation: the fact that everyone, no matter how good his life seems, has the same basic problems with which to contend. Everyone gets hurt in social contacts; everyone grows older and suffers; and everyone is uncertain about his future. The fact of being human creates certain special problems, as the existentialists have repeatedly pointed out. Perceiving the very real problems in himself, the mature person has a special feeling for others who have the same problems. Despite wide differences in life situations, natural gifts, and personal problems, everyone has much in common. No one is the complete master of his destiny—all must face many unknowns.

Allport held the view that even if the great religions had not emphasized brotherly love as being one of man's noblest achievements, the mature among us would certainly have set an example. We can live without warm social relationships; but we are talking about ideal living, not just survival. Because we are the way we are, it is unthinkable that there could be fulfillment in life without warm social relationships.

Emotional Security

The mature person accepts his emotions as a natural and vital part of himself, neither allowing them to rule his life nor putting the lid on them by overcontrol, denial, or distortion. He not only learns to live with his emotions, he uses them for constructive purposes. For example, an angry person can convert the extra emotional energy into constructive behavior. Some of the world's greatest accomplishments were the product of strong emotions. Strong feelings about racial injustices led to violent behavior, and then to civil rights laws. But strong emotions may cause us to behave like demented savages; thus many people come to fear their emotions. Their emotions are like a foreign element that threatens to take over the personality. The immature person may easily play out his emotions on others: If he is upset, everyone around him knows it and suffers. The mature person learns to live with his moods, continues normal activities, and above all, does not inflict his bad disposition on others. The emotionally secure person has gained emotional control, that is, he can trust his emotions because he knows that he has control of them. In this sense, he is much more self-accepting than is the average person who typically fears his emotions. Allport held that expressing emotions freely is a dangerous and risky business, and that we ought to be quite certain that we are not "poisoning the air that others have to breathe." Like explosive energy, our emotions can get away from us and become destructive. But all useful energy should be harnessed—and released—according to the amount of work that has to be done.

Realistic Perception

Some psychologists believe that perception is the key to a healthy or maladjusted life style. Perception is the first step in the behavior chain; and if it is distorted, then everything else—needs, emotions, goal-seeking behavior—will be inappropriate. A person who has a general habit of seeing things pessimistically will perceive and interpret events in a gloomy way. If one has a long standing expectation that other people will find him unattractive, he will see evidence of this all around him in his social relationships. We bring into every situation a vast store of past experience; and it is easy to misperceive, to exaggerate, or underestimate danger, and so on. Under the best circumstances, we have difficulty arriving at a correct view of things; but the person who is overly defensive, suspicious, or hypersensitive is easily the victim of misperception. How often have you puzzled about the remarks of a friend: Was he joking this morning, or could he have been serious? Later, when we discover that he is just as friendly as ever, we wonder whatever possessed us to doubt the friendship.

Useful Skills

The mature person has useful skills. He can usually meet the necessities of life rather easily, so that his attention can be directed to the priceless unessentials. If a person has to devote all his time and effort just to keeping body and soul together, he can hardly do the sort of things that would make for maturity. The free use of our abilities gives pleasure, and the perfecting of skills can be a lifetime endeavor. When is the concert pianist satisfied that he has reached perfection? When is the skilled writer totally pleased with his work? Exercising a skill easily and well is one of the greatest joys of life. A retired group of executives have formed a club to help struggling young companies because, as one spokesman pointed out, "If you enjoy solving problems, you want to go on solving them."

We often do not think of social activities as skills; but social skills, in a sense, underlie most other skills. In practically everything we do, we are involved with people, and getting along with them is essential in meeting our needs. The mature person is one who meets his needs comfortably and well.

Worthwhile Assignments

The most valuable thing we have is our time, and fortunately, we are all equal in that, because everyone has the same number of hours in a day. How we occupy our time is one of the key factors in maturity. Many people have the idea that idleness is the ideal state for man. Many people who suffered the hardships of the great depression of the 1930s yearned for retirement when they did not have to work. Undoubtedly, many jobs are routine, boring, debilitating, and just plain backbreaking. It is equally true that having meaningful things to do, or having a job with which one identifies, is one of the best ways to spend time. Work brings out many aspects of the self: self-extension, self-esteem, self-image, self as a problem-solver, self as a striver after goals. Thus, satisfying work can be as fulfilling as any other human pursuit. A life of leisure and indulgence is not the best road to happiness. Many people who have these things are desperate for something useful to do.

Being Objective About Self

Just as having a correct perception of things external to us makes a big difference in total adjustment, so also is having a correct view of ourselves essential for the good life. Knowing ourselves involves three aspects: (1) knowing what we can now do; (2) knowing what we cannot do; and (3) knowing what we ought to do. How many people set their goals too high or too low for their potentialities? How many people are a mystery to themselves? They cannot even specify what they want in life, although they may have a hundred complaints of what is wrong with things.

Guiding Purpose, Goals, Values

Contrast the person who has no clearly defined goals and who lives only by momentary desires with the person who has a strongly held religion which gives meaning to his life. Many different behaviors may be made meaningful by the pursuit of a guiding goal, as in the case of a man who strives vigorously for vocational success in order to adequately support his family. However, we should not think of a guiding purpose in glamorous terms. Some people find the ordinary things of everyday life full of meaning and value. A hardworking house painter may strive to please his favorite customers. The high point of his job is the compliment he receives when the job is well done. A man may find great satisfaction in working to support his family. Getting his children through school and college keeps him going. Living with a purpose is an important requirement of maturity. Many successful people report that interest in, and satisfaction with, their work for its own sake is what gives their lives direction. We can expect young people to have some trouble with their long-term goals because they go through a period of uncertainty and confusion; thus maturity usually does not occur before the thirties, when one begins to settle on his life's goals.

Maturity and Happiness

If we accept Allport's standards for maturity, it should be evident that having the qualities he mentioned would provide many satisfactions and joys. Yet Allport held that happiness and maturity are not the same. Happiness is probably an unattainable goal, if it is taken as mental tranquility, euphoria, or being "turned on." Many people's lives are filled with hardship and sorrow. Happiness could hardly describe the lives of such people; but maturity, taken in the sense of a certain orientation to life, is certainly a much more attainable goal. We may be victims of circumstances over which we have no control; but we can surely control our reactions to them—the way we perceive and respond to them. Happiness is, perhaps, only for a heavenly place; but we can hope to approach life in a mature way.

The Fully
Functioning Person:
Carl Rogers

8

Carl R. Rogers was born in 1902 in Oak Park, Illinois. He trained as a psychologist, and has become world known for his client-centered therapy. He is currently involved with the growth movement, which is a movement which seeks to promote effective living, and group therapy. He was a pioneer in opening psychotherapy to scrutiny by recording what took place in the psychotherapeutic consulting room. He wished to shed light on the processes that take place when counseling or personality therapy is successful or unsuccessful. Examining his numerous recorded sessions led Rogers to the conclusion that the people who came to him with personality problems were actually trying to find their real selves. The most common complaint was that life seemed artificial and unreal; and often the person felt that he was nothing but a hollow shell. He seemed to be what others wanted, rather than a real and vital agent in his own right. Rogers found that he could be of greatest help in providing a warm, accepting, and free atmosphere, so that the person felt free to look within himself. Self-discovery and self-expression emerged as the two major objectives of this new client-centered therapy.

Rogers became associated with permissiveness, with respect for the individual, and with the idea that everyone had a right to be unique. Like any growing thing, the human being requires favorable conditions in order to support his growth tendencies. These tendencies are inherent in the individual and do not have to be forced. Superiors should not try to live the lives of their subordinates. Rogers advocated profound respect for personal individuality, whether in a client, a patient, an employee, a student, or a child. Those who have power over others often abuse the amount of control they exercise. For instance, Rogers would point out that parents do not own their children. The growing child has a right to become a person of his own making. Yet how many parents try to force their children into marriages, vocations, and life styles which they, the parents, desire.

Rogers has promoted such ideas as expanded consciousness, emotional freedom, and the enjoyment of a rich inner life. He has encouraged his clients and students to follow their own ways rather than the directions which others have forced upon them. Rogers describes his ideal person, the fully functioning person, in the usual way as happy, blissful, content, and joyful; but he adds other qualities to highlight the highest human functions—such as living that is exciting, challenging, rewarding, and meaningful. The fully functioning person attempts to live life fully through freedom, creativity, and spontaneity in self-expression.

BASIC CONCEPTS AND PRINCIPLES

Need for Positive Regard

Rogers strongly believes that we all need the care of at least a few people. Because a young child has such limited contacts, this need is extremely important. All of us, especially the young child, often have to meet certain standards of conduct in order to receive the positive concern and acceptance of those who are important to us. The fulfillment of these conditions, particularly when they are quite contrary to a person's natural tendencies, starts the process of faulty personality growth. For example, the child who is taught that anger is wrong is put in the impossible position of having to deny a natural tendency in himself. If many of his impulses are denied, a very dangerous process—the loss of contact with vital aspects of personality—occurs. Eventually, the very center of personality, the self, becomes actually unreal. The person begins to think of himself in ways that are out of touch with his real feelings and tendencies. There is a striking resemblance between Rogers' views of the development of abnormal personality and those of Karen Horney, who stressed the alienation process, the loss of contact with the real self.

Conditions of Worth

We might further explore the process of developing a false conception of self by considering Rogers' notion of conditions of worth. As we have noted, to receive the positive regard of certain people, we have to meet certain conditions, which Rogers calls conditions of worth. When a mother says to her young child, "Good Johnny, make all gone," she is imposing a condition of worth in telling her child that he is good if he eats all his food. There is nothing wrong with conditions of worth, because the child has to learn certain ways of doing things to succeed in life; but when these conditions of worth are highly idealistic, or impossible to fulfill, they help to develop a false self-conception.

Any person who is meaningful to us has the power to set conditions of worth. Consider the father who will only regard straight As as an acceptable standard. In encouraging the child to learn certain skills and attitudes, a teacher may impose impossible conditions of worth. Only a few children may meet the standards of performance that are set. Honors and rewards are really forms of conditions of worth, and are given for achievement, irrespective of natural gifts and advantages. Most people do not meet the standards. Is it any wonder that many people dislike school?

External conditions of worth often become internal. We gradually take over the standards, or conditions of worth, imposed by others and begin to think of them as our own standards. When this occurs, the person becomes his own taskmaster. He may believe that he is a worthy person only if he is loved by everyone, or only if he makes a lot of money, or only if he can keep his emotions under control, and so on. The higher the standards, the greater the likelihood of failure. But standards are not easily changed, and often a person encounters evidence of failure in fulfilling his ideal standards. Thus, rather than changing standards, the person utilizes the process of distortion to block out or lessen the force of the evidence. For example, if one's emotions challenge the standards of perfection, the emotions must be prevented from being sensed. If certain drives are unacceptable, these also are subject to denial and repression. The false self-concept is to be maintained at all costs. Given the choice between changing the self-concept or denying both external and internal information, many people cling to the false self-concept because they fear the loss of positive regard from others and of their own self-esteem.

Self-Concept

We have noted that there are many causes of our behavior. The ringing telephone is annoying, and so we answer it. If I am hungry, I begin to think of some way of obtaining food. For Rogers, the most important cause of behavior is our self-concept. What you think of yourself plays a part in practically everything you do. The person who thinks of himself as loving, kind, considerate, and attractive thinks, feels, and acts in ways that are consistent with this conception of self. He expects to be treated by others with respect and acceptance. A person who has an unfavorable conception of himself may find that his behavior follows and agrees with this conception of self. He may believe that he is unattractive, unlovable, and uninteresting; and he may act accordingly. Parents, teachers, and Sunday School masters sometimes present such an unrealistic model for the child that the child always falls short. If this model is accepted by the child as the ideal self, then his real self will fall far short of the ideal self. If this happens, he may come to believe that he is basically evil and inferior. We sometimes observe in the same person a concept of self that is both favorable and unfavorable: The person may actually believe that he is rather extraordinary and that he possesses many desirable attributes, but at the same time, he may also see himself as nasty, selfish, and hateful. At any given time, one conception predominates and controls behavior; but the other is in the background and may come to the fore unexpectedly.

Putting on a Mask

We all work to develop a social personality in order to make a favorable impression on others. Yet there may be a serious inconsistency between this social personality and what we really are. Most of us are aware that we try to be appealing to some people but that we behave quite differently with others. Rogers makes an interesting observation about the discrepancy between the social personality and what one really thinks he is: What a person thinks of himself—and this is often quite unfavorable—is not actually the real self either. In such instances, the fact is that the person does not really know his true self. A college student who is busy impressing people all day long may be quite harsh with a younger brother. The student may feel guilty at times concerning his behavior because he perceives the discrepancy; but the real self is neither the social personality nor the harsh, nasty big brother. An important point is that this discrepancy exists in part because the person has not discovered his true self. He does not really know who he is; thus his behavior lacks consistency.

We learn early in life that we simply cannot behave as we wish, but that we must meet certain expectations. The student who does not feel at his best cannot simply decide to quit working on his math test. If a young person gets angry with his parents, he can create quite a problem for himself by free expression. If we feel irritable and tense, we might get impatient with others; but, again, repeated harsh experience has taught us to hold back on our true feelings. Many people come to fear their natural impulses and feelings, and they try to be calm or composed all the time, or always cheerful and noncomplaining. Although holding back on negative emotions is essential for living effectively, frequently we go too far and begin to develop an artificial personality. We begin to put on a mask that we take for the real self. Usually the mask fits some cultural model or parental expectations, but it does not allow the true self to come out. As we have noted, to live out this concept of self, many aspects of the personality have to be denied, distorted, or kept from awareness. Even external information has to be selectively interpreted and filtered. The person cannot even trust his senses.

ABNORMAL TYPES

Freud characterized the neurotic as being oversocialized, by which he meant that the conscience was too critical. Too much is expected of self and of others, and the person develops a host of defensive measures in order to protect himself from his short-comings and failures. Rogers takes a different view: No matter what the particular symptoms are, abnormalities are ultimately the result of a faulty self-concept. This self-concept develops through faulty life experiences.

One person may always look outside of himself for standards, and so he never knows what his true self really is. Another person adopts a compliant style of relating to others, so that he does not risk being disapproved. He gives up the most basic desires of his self for the sake of positive regard from others. Some people are so ashamed of what they consider their true selves that they play-act all the time. They become so involved in their various roles that the real self is not experienced. A common form of abnormal person-ality is the person who is driven by "musts" and "shoulds," keeping his own feelings and desires constantly under control, or not even felt. These people never feel comfortable inside because they always fall short of the artificial standards which they have accepted as their own values. In all these instances, we can see that the major disturbance behind all the symptoms is the false self-concept. Rather than dealing directly with the various symptoms, Rogers has found that helping the person discover his true self is the best approach. When this discovery occurs, the symptoms disappear.

We Are Players

We are all forced into certain roles, whether we like it or not. A role is a way of acting. These are usually external to us, that is, they are a part of our particular culture or subculture. The culture tells us what is expected of a mother, a teacher, an adult, an elderly person, and of the various positions that we occupy. The role can vary somewhat, but generally, it involves certain dos and don'ts. For example, mothers are expected to love and support their children, not abuse and neglect them.

Everyone actually occupies several roles, depending on age, sex, social status, vocation, and other types of class characteristics. Sometimes we become so caught up in our roles that we have difficulty discovering our real self. We may find ourselves changing roles so frequently that we do not know what is most typical of our self. One of the major tasks of living, in Rogers' view, is to discover and express the self in the various roles that we must carry out. We may over-identify with a particular role; but we may also go to the opposite extreme and reject the various roles of our culture. Both of these approaches are abnormal responses to the task of harmonizing our real self with the various roles that we take on.

Another significant problem related to roles is the matter of learning what they are. As important as roles are in our lives, they are not taught or communicated in a systematic way. No one tells the young adult just exactly what to do or not to do to fit into his job, his social group, or his dating role. One may fail repeatedly in his various settings as a result of his lack of adequate role understanding or performance. The aspiring young executive may not sense what is expected of him; thus he fails to progress in his job. His difficulty is the inability to learn his role.

Aside from the problem of learning roles, how can we still be ourselves and carry out the various roles that form a part of our lives? We surely cannot behave with our parents in the same way as with an old school friend, a sweetheart, or a boss. A part of the answer is that we can carry out our roles well or poorly. A child may try to assume the role of an adult with his parents; consequently his relationship with them is strained and fraught with friction. He is not following the role of a child very well. One way to live successfully is to learn to sense our various roles and to perform them as well as possible. The roles we carry out must express qualities of the real self, and not artificial poses for the sake of meeting someone else's expectations.

Rogers believes that we must extend the real self into our various roles. We can still be thoughtful, generous, self-protecting, and honest in all our various roles. The core qualities of the self can be maintained.

The major difficulty is discovering this real self. As Rogers points out, what appears to the person to be the real self may be a distorted conception of the self. The indications are obvious: The person experiences all sorts of internal and external symptoms— stress, confusion, frustration, lack of acceptance, chronic dissatisfaction, and a variety of aches and pains.

Emotional Disturbance

It appears that when things go wrong in personality development or functioning, the emotions and feelings are most affected. Our emotion is the part of us that is most injured in a poor school or home environment. When attempts to express genuine emotions, either positive or negative, are met with punishment and frustration, the person begins to deny or repress them. If emotions repeatedly cause trouble for us, we might respond by trying to do away with them altogether; but of course, this means cutting off vital aspects of our personality. It also means becoming an artificial person. The milder reactions to this loss of contact with emotions are feelings of being trapped, of being guarded, or of being restricted and limited. The more serious reactions include feelings of unreality, a sense of being superficial, and a sense of not having any identity. The person may complain of feeling empty, and of not participating genuinely in life. An essential ingredient of self-exploration is a sensing of feelings and emotions, even those that are negative and most unflattering to the person. Negative feelings toward parents may be difficult to accept as one's own; but they are better felt than covered over because at least one knows that he has them, and can take steps to change conditions by confronting his parents. But denial and distortion can only make matters worse.

Psychological Breakdown

As we have noted, the person with a false conception of self has to cut off vital experiences—both those coming from within himself and those coming from the external world. A protective system of defenses is formed in order to preserve the concept of self. Occasionally, the correct impressions get through the defenses; and then the person may experience a psychological breakdown or a great deal of anxiety.

Suppose a young man conceives of himself as being brave and unafraid, but that, in a situation which threatens his life, he panics and loses control of himself. Now he is faced with evidence that contradicts his conception of self, but he cannot deny it; thus he may experience a terrible sense of confusion and stress. He is now faced with his own cowardice, and this is extremely unacceptable to him. He may respond in a number of ways: For one thing, he may simply recover from the shock and further increase his defenses so that he can preserve his false self-concept. This means further distortion of personality, and also the greater likelihood that he will encounter his unacceptable behavior again. On the other hand, he may perceive the need to change his self-concept.

Rogers has found that, in a warm and permissive counseling climate where the person feels free to express himself, more and more of the personality becomes open to inspection. At first the process is painful because the person does not want to learn certain things about his self; but gradually, as one goes beyond these unpleasant aspects, one finds things about himself that are quite acceptable and even praiseworthy. For the first time in his life, the person may actually find something about himself to like and appreciate. But is this restricted only to a counseling setting? The answer, according to Rogers, is "no."

The same things that take place in counseling can occur in a warm and accepting friendship. An understanding and accepting friend can help us to explore ourselves. When the person feels free to express his innermost feelings, then certain aspects of personality which have been blocked off will begin to emerge into consciousness and become a part of the concept of self. The self-concept then becomes what the person really is. What the person believes himself to be corresponds to what the person really is.

IDEAL PERSONALITY AND LIVING

Rogers details the attributes of the fully functioning person; and we may consider them as consisting of a model of ideal personality and living. Although Rogers would claim universality for them, these attributes are probably more compatible with certain personality types than others.

Process Living

Process living means to be willing to take a dynamic and flexible orientation to life. The opposite approach is a static or fixed style of life, such as always following the conservative interpretation, meeting fixed standards of achievement, or following rigid standards of conduct. We may think that attaining certain goals such as marriage, job status, and social acclaim will produce happiness, but one never attains a static state of bliss once and for all. Growing up, marriage, and job status are not really end points but turning points. Marriage requires constant adjustments, as the two partners change with age. Successful performance on a job requires continual adaptation to new circumstances. Growing up is a continuing process.

Process living means that a person is willing to flow with his experiences. He does not impose an order and meaning on his experiences, but rather lets his experiences direct him. Contrary to process living are fixed ideas of interpreting and doing things— from a liberal point of view, a selfish orientation, a Republican or Democratic view, and so forth.

According to Rogers, the good life is not a destination which is simply attained, but rather a style of living in which the person participates fully in life. It is a continual process of becoming. An essential feature of this orientation is inner freedom and a continuing evaluation of the directions one follows. If he follows cultural standards, it is because they are compatible with his own nature and goals.

Finally, process living means that we focus on the present, and attempt to derive as much as we can in the here and now. We should not continually relive past conflicts and problems, as so many do. We should also not make the attainment of goals in the future so important that the present is always simply a means. It is the present moment that we must live fully, even as we reach toward the future.

Openness to Experience

Making more of the personality conscious and opening all channels of information describes the quality of openness to experience. As we have noted, painful experience causes the self-concept to be formed in a distorted way. Openness to internal and external experience may expose one to hurt and to unpleasant truths about self, but at least the person can make necessary changes and can perhaps follow a different course of meeting needs. The person who really does not have musical talent is better off learning this unwelcome information about himself rather than vainly pursuing an endeavor that will only cause repeated frustration. You cannot continue to live a lie without having the awful truth brought home to you at some point.

A person who is open to himself and to his sensory inputs has more information on which to base his judgments and decisions. We might think of a computer which is directed to carry on certain calculations with only partial information. Obviously, conclusions and decisions based on partial evidence are less likely to be correct or useful. Openness to experience is a matter of degree. Some people are ready to take in most of what is going on inside and outside themselves. They simply get more out of themselves and their environment. Furthermore, they are not hampered by preconceptions and prejudices. Their guiding assumptions about people and things are not held so rigidly that they cannot be changed. In fact, one of the basic assumptions of an open person is to be willing to let go of the old for a better prospect.

Behaving as One Feels Like Behaving

Rogers believes that we ought to be trusting enough in ourselves to follow intuitions and feelings. The opposite of this is to assemble all relevant information, to ponder all possible consequences, and finally, after arduous weighing of choices, to take a course of action. The person who tries to be superrational may end up choosing nothing and continuing in his unpleasant conditions. Rogers does not mean that one should make hasty choices and judgments without having sufficient information or adequate deliberation, but rather that one should trust enough in the self to follow intuitions and feelings. Sometimes one must trust his total response to a situation more than simply his intellectual reaction. The decision, when it emerges, may feel like it came out of the blue, but it is more like a conclusion based on evidence which is not totally in one's mind. Many creative people have reported that they frequently approach a difficult problem by gathering information that is necessary for a solution, and then turning away from the problem altogether. Many instances of spontaneous solutions are recorded. Learning about the self can lead to trust in one's intuitions. Feelings can be acted upon. When the person is fully functioning, it appears that the total organism is wiser than the knowing powers alone.

Sense of Freedom

The fully functioning person feels that he has choices, and that he is in control of his destiny. The opposite quality is the feeling of being trapped, of having one's life lived for him. A person who is dominated by "musts" and "shoulds" feels hemmed-in on all sides. For Rogers, the fully functioning person certainly has guiding principles and values, but they are an integral part of his self-concept. They are not like Freud's idea of a superego that watches over the ego; rather, the guiding ideals are an essential part of the self. Although firmly established, the guiding ideals of the fully functioning person are replaceable, so that even when circumstances change, or the person changes, new values and guiding principles are adopted. The fully functioning person is willing to change his concepts and principles because he knows that living is a dynamic process. Our concepts and principles are devices to help us meet the problems of living; but a rigid set of ideas can only hinder personality functioning and hamper a sense of freedom. When we are functioning fully, we will experience our needs and emotions as they are and not as some artificial standard dictates. We will also let our experiences of the external world speak for themselves. With this free flow of information, the chances of satisfying our needs and dealing effectively with our circumstances are certainly much greater than when we force information into fixed interpretations or block it out altogether. We feel free because we have more options.

Spontaneity and Creativity

Spontaneity and creativity flow naturally from the other attributes of the fully functioning person. Free expression of the self may require the willingness to give up security and to go against the opinion of loved ones. Rather than seeking to make his life predictable, safe, orderly, and without tensions, the fully functioning person enjoys new experiences, challenges, the joy of the moment, and even relishes stimulation and excitement. We might describe him as being psychologically mobile, and this is a good condition for spontaneity and creative living. Running in narrow tracks and just getting by does not describe the fully functioning person.

The following analogy may help to convey Rogers's notion of the differences between the fully functioning person and the typical individual. The fully functioning car glides easily up and down hills, and efficiently hums along. It is quieter, more efficient in fuel consumption, and wears out less rapidly. On the other hand, the car which is out of tune, and sputters along with much effort and noise, can barely get where it's going—and on top of it all, it ages prematurely. Fixed paths, goals that cannot be abandoned, standards that cannot be changed—all these are not conducive to creative living. The human being, when functioning fully, is creative and dynamic. He enjoys change and novelty; and in fact, he works to produce it.

The good life, according to Rogers, is characterized by a wide range of experience. One should strive for rich new experiences, a variety of human contacts, and free use of one's abilities. Above all, one should learn to be in touch with his emotions and feelings, and to express them sensitively. Rogers believes that we can all be "a trustworthy instrument for encountering life." The good life is not for the timid and security-bound because it requires courage to face problems, to grow in one's experiences. It means having to tolerate uncertainty, confusion, and even pain. Growth is painful at times because we have to give up the things that count with us, as when a young woman gives up her parental home for the uncertainties of marriage, for example. But the good life also means being free to be oneself, enjoying rich experiences, and fulfilling the potentialities of growth with which one is born.

Changes That Take Place in Successful Counseling

Rogers attempts to help us understand the fully functioning person by pointing out the changes that take place in clients who respond well to counseling. Examining such changes in personality and behavior should bring out the characteristics of both abnormal and normal or ideal growth and functioning. Counseling is like a piece of living, which involves learning. While we do not all need counseling, we can all learn from living. We learn many things such as new words, new skills, and new ideas through memorization; but the type of learning involved in the art of living requires experiences such as loving someone. It includes discovery of self, increasing one's capacity to sense, increased spontaneity and creativity, and positive regard for self. Rogers firmly believes that personality changes are not brought about by memorizing principles of mental health, or by obtaining an analysis of one's abnormalities, or simply by learning a prescribed set of guidelines. Rogers believes that hardships are involved in personality change, and that such hardships are overcome by suffering them and by learning to live through them.

Here are some of the kinds of learning that take place in successful counseling, as reported by Rogers.

1. The person comes to see himself differently.
2. He accepts himself and his feelings more fully.
3. He becomes more self-confident and self-directing.
4. He becomes more the person he would like to be.
5. He becomes more flexible, less rigid in his perception.
6. He adopts more realistic goals for himself.
7. He behaves in a more mature fashion.
8. He changes his maladjusted behaviors, even such a long-established one as chronic alcoholism.
9. He becomes more accepting of others.
10. He becomes more open to evidence about what is going on outside of himself as well as what is happening inside himself.
11. He changes his basic personality characteristics in constructive ways.[1]

Portrait of the Fully Functioning Person

The following list of attributes and behaviors should convey the picture of the fully functioning person, according to Rogers' model of personality: self-aware, creative; spontaneous; open to

---

[1]Carl Rogers, *On Becoming a Person* (Boston: Houghton Mifflin, 1961), pp. 80-81.

experience, self-accepting; self-determined; free from rigid standards; lives fully in the moment; allows full expression of potentialities; trusts his organism; has a firm sense of identity; avoids fronts and artificial poses; has a sense of inner freedom; his values are his own; he is willing to experience living as a process or as a continual state of becoming; and he flows with experience. If these qualities seem quite idealistic to you, bear in mind that Rogers is referring to a normal personality that is fully developed and fully functioning—an understandably small percentage of the population now, but an idealistic state that is obtainable.

The Self-Actualizing Person: Abraham Maslow

9

Maslow (1908-1970) was one of the pioneers in the humanistic psychology movement. He stressed a health and growth psychology. He was primarily concerned with the highest potentialities of man, both collectively and individually. In his view, personality therapists had concentrated too long on personality disorders and the abnormal. Such preoccupation with abnormalities led to a one-sided emphasis—just get rid of the symptoms somewhat, and help the victim of personality disorders to live better than he did with his symptoms. However, what were considered cures by the personality therapists were really milder, or less obvious, forms of abnormalities.

Maslow was mainly concerned with the very large group of people who functioned on a much lower level than their potential warranted. Such people did not have typical personality disorders, as judged according to the standards of serious psychological illnesses, but fell far short of full development and optimum functioning. These failures in the art of living did not result in confinement in a psychiatric ward, or even in consultation with a personality therapist. Maslow would argue that they were not considered abnormal by experts or by themselves; but according to what Maslow saw as the highest possibilities for man, these failures were certainly abnormal. Maslow sought to study the highest levels of human attainment with respect to personality growth and functioning. He wanted to bring out the full possibilities of man in his model of ideal personality growth and development. He argued that we should study the best specimens, the most evolved, and the most perfect humans in order to construct our model. His standard for normality was full development and optimum functioning; anything less than that implied reverting to the standard of health as lack of illness rather than as fulfillment.

Maslow studied people who, he felt, were stars in the art of living. Such persons are rare and difficult to study. Maslow himself was often very surprised by some of his findings. Even the healthiest of people did not fit the common view of the perfected human being; they were not heartyextroverts, disarming, always agreeable, charming, and loving. They were actually quite self-sufficient and inner-directed.

Maslow's humanistic psychology is wide-ranging. He was always a keen observer of his times. He felt that our cultural institutions were based on a distorted conception of man's nature. The prevailing view which underlies child-rearing practices, formal education, and even our major religions, is that man is animalistic and utterly self-centered in his most natural state. That view holds that only strict discipline and the continual threat of punishment can hold these tendencies in their proper place. Maslow felt that gratifications rather than the denial and the restriction of basic needs would bring out the best in man. He believed that allowing freedom of expression and supporting the developing person so that full potentialities could be expressed would produce a different race of human beings.

BASIC CONCEPTS AND PRINCIPLES

Different Need Levels

Maslow stressed the place of needs in his model of personality. He distinguished among various major classes of needs, such as the dynamic, the cognitive, and the aesthetic needs. Dynamic needs are involved in the maintenance of our body, our social relationships, our need for success and respect from others, and our most personal desires, talents, and aspirations. Cognitive needs are associated with knowing and making sense of the things we observe. Aesthetic needs have to do with the appreciation of beauty, of order, and of sensory experiences. These various needs are the most essential features of our personality, and they account for most of our behavior. We will discuss what occurs when they are, or are not, properly gratified. Maslow believed that the best thing to do with any need is to gratify it, unless, of course, the need is a harmful learned craving, such as addictive drugs or alcohol.

Physiological Needs. The most powerful needs are those which support the operations of the body. These are felt as strong drives such as hunger, thirst, pain avoidance, or sexual tension. Maslow described these physiological drives as prepotent, which means that they take priority over everything else. If you are very hungry or thirsty, or if you are in severe pain, nothing is important except relief. One does not think about his status in the community, his unhappy love life, or his unfulfilled talents when he is under the control of a potent drive such as hunger, or when he feels a severe pain that threatens his very existence. We noted above that some physiological needs are felt; some, on the other hand, are not. You do not experience a craving for potassium, although the body needs it; this is also true of other vital food substances. Lacking a sufficient balance of vitamins and minerals, the body may become disordered without your awareness of the missing ingredient. Maslow made an interesting observation about the highest human needs that parallels this point: That is, we often do not know what is wrong with us, even though a vital need is being frustrated.

A curious thing about all felt needs is that satisfaction of them results in pleasure; thus eating, drinking, reducing pain, and releasing sexual tension give pleasure. Many people try to attain happiness by indulging their physiological needs—more and better food, drink, sex, sensual stimulation, and so on. Wouldn't it be wonderful to eat steak every night, to have a different sex partner each time, to quench one's thirst by tantalizing alcoholic beverages? The average person does not simply eat to survive, but seeks to indulge his appetite. Maslow did not deny the lower needs; rather, he stressed that they are not the only important needs for men. In fact, the higher needs, those which appear to be most distinctively human, actually give pleasure which is more enduring and of greater intensity. Maslow rejected the exclusive preoccupation with lower need gratification.

Safety Needs.   Safety needs are next in importance, and are very powerful in many people's lives. Just as some people focus most of their attention on their basic biological requirements, so many people are most concerned about safety, security, and a predictable future. Everyone has the fear of not being able to make it, of not being able to support himself as an independent person. In a complex society such as ours, there is much to learn and many things to overcome. Fear of failure in the important tasks of life is a major concern for all of us. Having the ability to project into the future, to anticipate the terrible things that could happen, makes it quite easy to exaggerate these possibilities. Often, the only thing we can do is to take whatever safeguards that are open to us, and then trust that things will go our way. Life is still very insecure for many people, particularly for the adolescent and young adult.

A sense of security is partly psychological because it is based upon interpretations of circumstances. Furthermore, everyone must deal with unknowns and an unpredictable future. No matter how bright, wealthy, or attractive one might be, he still cannot control unforeseen events. Some people seem to be capable of living with uncertainties, while others find them almost impossible to bear. Part of the difference is due to different interpretations of things. A painful experience may be taken as a sign of inferiority and weakness for one person, but another may interpret the same experience as a painful but valuable lesson. Of course, security does depend on external supports, but the dependence is not as direct as many people think. Some people who have very little security have been able to move on to higher needs.

Love and Belonging Needs. Maslow held, in common with some other personality scientists, that man is by nature a social creature. We like and love other people and want them to like and love us. The healthy person has several levels of personal involvement with others; in general, there is a strong need to fit in, or belong to a particular group—more typically to several groups. When physiological and safety needs are at least partially met, the major concern is being liked, accepted, loved, and being considered attractive by others. One only need listen to a few popular songs to appreciate the role love and belonging needs play in our lives. The obsessive preoccupation with romantic love arises not only because of the operation of love and belonging needs, but because of the powerful sex drive—which is a basic physiological need.

Everyone has a number of social settings in which he willingly or unwillingly participates, so that the desire to belong and to be an acceptable member is frequently activated. A person may feel unwanted, unacceptable, and even unlovable as a result of such encounters. We do not normally undergo formal training in social skills, but such learning is extremely valuable in the developing person. So much depends upon the gratification of the love and belonging needs that a person might be scarred for life as a result of their frustration. Being accepted in important social settings and groups is essential for attaining the still higher levels of need gratification.

Esteem Needs. The need for esteem involves other people. No one wants to be considered incompetent, lacking in skills, or unworthwhile. Esteem means the respect and valuation of others. It involves a sense of dignity, of competence and mastery, of being as good as anyone else. We not only want to be acceptable to the important people around us, but we also want to be known for certain attributes and achievements, such as our vocation, skills, talents, and our fine character traits. We often select one outstanding characteristic of ourselves that best describes us, such as being a nice guy, a hard worker, witty or charming. These attributes support a sense of esteem. Eventually we develop self-acceptance, self-respect, and self-love, which are the highest expression of the esteem needs.

Self-Actualizing Needs.   Maslow referred to the highest human needs as the self-actualizing or growth needs because their gratification leads to expansion of the self and to the increase of involvement and activity. The highest human needs are not even experienced until the lower needs are at least partially gratified. The higher needs may easily be over-ridden by the much stronger lower needs or by certain learned cravings. One is functioning at the highest level when he is doing what is important to himself, what he really wants to do, or what he experiences as being most expressive of his self. It need not be what the culture considers creative or productive; rather, it may be a very personal matter—being a good mother or father, being able to make music, or write, or build things.

What Do Growth Needs Feel Like?   Self-actualizing people report that when they are functioning at the highest level of growth needs they feel at the peak of their powers; they are able to operate smoothly, effectively, and effortlessly. They report feeling more intelligent, more perceptive, wittier, stronger, and more graceful than at other times. They do not waste effort fighting and restraining themselves. They feel themselves fully responsible, creative, and in total control.

These inward qualities cannot occur without external manifestation. Such individuals appear to others to be effective, decisive, strong, single-minded, and able to overcome opposition. To the observer they appear self-assured, more trustworthy, reliable, and dependable. Maslow tried to create an impressionistic portrait of a fully self-actualized person by the following colorful description: Spontaneity, expressiveness, innocence, naivety, candidness, childlikeness, unguardedness, defenselessness, naturalness, simplicity, responsiveness, unhesitant manner, plainness, sincerity, unaffectedness, primitiveness, freely flowing outwardness, instinctiveness, unrestrainedness, unself-consciousness.

Such descriptive categories of personality traits may be the rating scales of the future, when we know a lot more about the highest human potentialities and how to fulfill them. Most rating scales now deal with qualities that are related to lower need functioning.

Knowing as Needs. Maslow also assigned to our knowing capabilities the status of needs. The normal person is curious about his world and himself. He has a need to explore, to understand, to organize, and to systematize things. When knowledge is inadequate or distorted he may feel suspicious and uneasy. Things do not just happen; there are reasons; and we have the apparatus to know and understand, to analyze and synthesize, and to put things into a system.

Needs for Beauty. We may not have considered the appreciation of beauty and pleasant sensory experiences as arising from a basic need, but Maslow believed that we do have what he termed aesthetic needs. Even the cave dwellers expressed this need in their artistic endeavors. We still have many examples of art work and pictures inscribed on the walls of caves. Like other needs, such needs are accompanied by pleasure when they are satisfied, and by tension when they are frustrated. People vary in the intensity of their aesthetic needs, which are expressed, like all needs, in individual ways. Thus, some people are actually disturbed by ugly surroundings, whereas other people are not bothered as much. Many people experience tension if their surroundings are unclean, disorderly, or inharmonious. One individual may feel an urge to straighten the crooked painting on the wall. Aesthetic needs are obviously not as strong and vital to life as the more basic needs; but again, although they are easily ignored, they constitute the flourish and the "something extra" that makes one life more interesting and dynamic than another.

Deficit Motivation Living Versus Growth Motivation Living. Maslow questioned whether we have our lives lived for us, or whether we have choices and can fulfill our deepest potentialities. He points out that many people are merely responders, reacting to external pressures, demands, requirements, and learned stimuli. Their lives are primarily reactions to emergencies, to pains and fears, to the demands of other people. How much of what we do is for our own enjoyment; how much occurs out of necessity? How much of what we do is preparing, or getting ready for some future thing; how much is doing what we must do? To enjoy beauty, to listen to great music, to be with good people—these experiences promote growth. Maslow observed that some people are always going but never arriving; they are always involved with means but they never get to the ends themselves.

He argued for what he called the B-life—living for itself—and not solely meeting deficits in ourselves or demands from the environment. For Maslow, "You can be better than you are" does not mean that you can suffer less from symptoms, but rather that you can live on a higher need level. Maslow believed that the healthiest people are foreign to the average person. Their motivations and personal experiences are truly on a different level, a level which most people experience only fleetingly, or not at all.

A thoughtful student may complain that so much concern with models of personality may be more harmful than good. Would it not be better to live a simple life without analyzing it? A working man does his uncomplicated job all day and comes home to his family, eats his supper, and watches television for the evening while consuming his favorite alcoholic beverage. His life is uncomplicated but pleasant—or so it would seem. Maslow would point out that many people who live in this manner are bored, restricted, and only half alive; their lives are routine and drab. They function on the lowest psychobiological level.

ABNORMAL TYPES

Need Frustration, the Major Cause of Abnormality

Although he recognized the role of stress and the significance of faulty development, Maslow was quite clear about the most important cause of abnormal personality: Abnormalities, he believed, are caused by basic need frustration. Even faulty development is generally caused by blocking of the basic needs. The child who is treated inconsistently by his parents does not find his world very safe and predictable. A child who is neglected by his parents may develop a profound sense of inferiority. Need frustration is the major factor in faulty personality growth, and it is also the major cause of abnormalities throughout life. The child may develop into a discipline problem because he does not get enough love. The adolescent may turn to crime because he lacks self-esteem. The young adult may feel unwanted because he does not fit in at work. The middle-aged person may feel that he is simply marking time, and that life is routine and boring. The elderly person may experience a depression because he has become isolated and useless to society.

Frustration of Physiological Needs

Our physiological needs are, of course, essential to life, and long-continued frustration may produce serious and irreparable illness. Protracted hunger, thirst, and deprivation of other physiological needs can create strong tensions and totally occupy the foreground of attention. Although we are often unclear about our higher needs, we are usually quite aware of the tensions of the lower needs. As powerful as they are, they are nevertheless capable of being distorted. One may eat for pleasure, rather than for sustenance. One may drink to produce a pleasant state of mind, rather than for quenching thirst. The satisfaction of physiological needs may be equated with happiness; thus many people become unduly preoccupied with them. But overeating is harmful to health, and excessive drinking of alcoholic beverages can produce serious physical and personality problems. Free sex, too, is not without its problems—unwanted pregnancies, venereal diseases, and perhaps a guilty conscience. Being tied to basic drive satisfaction is hardly the model life for Maslow, who so strongly believed that the higher needs are far more important for happiness than are the lower needs. But of course, Maslow did not pit higher against lower needs. He argued that we should put the lower needs in their place and move up to the higher needs.

Frustration of Safety Needs

Frustration of safety needs lies behind the development of many symptoms and personality disorders. For example, the compulsive neurotic tries to create order in his life by establishing and following fixed routines. Things have to be done in a certain way and at certain specified times. Ambiguity and uncertainty are so intolerable that the person uses desperate measures to avoid them. Other expressions of safety needs include believing in superstitious practices, such as clinging to good luck charms or uttering magical phrases. Many people might be described as victims of the struggle for security. They restrict their participation in life for the sake of security.

A particularly harmful approach is to avoid risks. Only the sure bet is accepted. The lives of such persons are characterized by need suppression and control rather than by gratification; for Maslow, this was the worst method of dealing with needs.

Frustration of Love and Belonging Needs

Frustration of love and belonging needs can cause severe personality disorders that can become chronic. A person may feel a total sense of rejection; he may feel that he does not fit into any of his social settings. Other people are a mystery, and he does not understand why he continually experiences difficulty in his social contacts. One of the most typical problems for the neurotic individual is friction in social relationships. He does not get along with people. It seems that he is always getting hurt, being discriminated against, and being misunderstood.

The greatest power on earth, said Erich Fromm, is the ability to love. Most people complain that they do not have enough of it. Children complain that their parents really do not care for them;

married couples complain about the lack of love and appreciation of the spouse; the employee feels that he really does not count for much with his boss. Many people are permanently rendered incapable of forming intimate relationships because they have suffered chronic frustration of the love and belonging needs.

Frustration of Esteem Needs

Low self-esteem means lack of self-worth—positive self-feelings. In the fierce competition of our society, one is often left to wonder about his status. Frustration and failures of basic needs make one feel inadequate and worthless. The complaint that ''I am not really good at anything'' is quite common. A profound sense of inferiority is found at the root of many personality disorders. Children are often made to feel small and insignificant in comparison with adults; but many adults never outgrow these feelings. They see almost everyone as being superior. Some forms of depression can be traced to a sense of low-esteem. One who carries a lot of shame and guilt feelings is also the victim of low self-esteem. How many people really feel loved enough by the ones they care about?

Frustration of the Growth Needs

As we have noted, Maslow was especially concerned about the types of illness that resulted from frustration of the higher needs. These disorders are widespread in modern civilizations because of the rapidity of life, the loss of rootedness, and the lack of enduring social contacts among people. Many of the disorders that the existentialists have identified are, in Maslow's need schema, the product of higher need frustration. Many people, for example, complain of lack of meaning in life. Nothing seems to make sense. Others find that they are not really interested in anything, and that nothing really counts or matters for them. Many complain of marking time, of routine living, of emptiness. Some people simply say that they are bored. Even with the easy availability of many luxuries, life has become quite drab and empty for many. Maslow believed that such conditions are caused by overpreoccupation with material possessions, with gratification of appetites, with status seeking, and with the other lower needs. Nothing is wrong with having the lower needs taken care of. In fact, these are essential for getting to the higher levels, the most subtle of needs. Gratification of all needs—dynamic, cognitive, or aesthetic—is essential for the good life.

IDEAL PERSONALITY AND LIVING

Traits of Self-Actualizing People

Maslow came to the conclusion that the level of functioning of self-actualizing people, whom he estimated constitute about one or two per cent of the population, is of a completely different order than is typical or considered normal. Self-actualizing people satisfy all their needs rather easily, but they are especially concerned about their higher needs.

Maslow even went so far as to say that a self-actualizing person becomes less American in style of life. He did not imply that self-actualizing people are radicals or extremists, but rather that they transcend any particular culture. Their humanness is fully developed. He identified a number of traits that characterized his self-actualizing subjects. Knowing such traits gives us a model of the possibilities for perfecting ourselves. All of us have the traits which Maslow noted, in some degree, and it should be possible to use Maslow's model as a portrait of perfected man.

More Efficient Perception of Reality, and More Comfortable Relationships With It.   Maslow found that his self-actualizing people had an uncanny ability to perceive the sham, the superficial, and the fake. Furthermore, they accepted reality without vain opposition to it. When we cooperate with the inevitables in life we can usually gain better control of the things that are open to us.

Acceptance of Self, Others, and Nature. Changing others to suit one's image often disturbs social relationships; but self-actualizing people respect the inherent right to be one's true self. Perceiving his own shortcomings, the self-actualizing person nevertheless accepts his essential self. He is not tormented by needless feelings of guilt and shame for falling short of cultural ideals of beauty, status, popularity, and so on. Self-actualizing people lack pretense, affectation, and a social front; and they are quick to sense these in others. They accept the natural changes with growth and do not hang onto old pleasures and modes of doing things.

Spontaneity, Simplicity, Naturalness. Being oneself requires a great deal of inner freedom and spontaneity. The opposite qualities include being guarded and cautious in self-expression, and constantly fearing the censorship of others. Self-actualizing people express themselves freely, easily, and with an air of confidence, but not in an irritating or snobbish manner. They do not play-act in dealing with others.

Problem Centering. Healthy people approach personal problems without intense emotions. Personal problems are treated like any other problem. The activity of solving problems gives special enjoyment to them and contributes to their vocational involvements as well.

As an example of problem-centering Maslow observed that an outstanding characteristic of the healthy person is a commitment to a vocation: He feels that his work is important, and that he has a mission in life, whether it be child-rearing or running a large corporation.

Need for Privacy. Many people find being alone with themselves an unpleasant experience, but Maslow found that his healthy subjects enjoyed their own experiences and actually sought privacy.

Autonomy. Healthy people are relatively independent of their environment, and are not victims of circumstantial changes over which they have no control. They are self-sufficient, and can rely on their own resources. They do not need the good opinion of other people to support them.

Continued Freshness of Appreciation. To be able to appreciate repeatedly the basic goods of life is an important characteristic of healthy people. The same event that might become boring and commonplace to less developed people is full of beauty, inspiration, and mystery to them. Unlike the average person, self-actualizers do not take the mysteries of life for granted. Furthermore, they are able to derive inspiration from what they already possess and from their previous accomplishments. They are not restlessly searching for newer and better things and excitements.

Mystic or Peak Experiences. Maslow found that many of his healthy subjects had strongly intense personal experiences that might be described as religious or mystical. An experience such as watching a child at play or listening to music could totally absorb their attention and produce a heightened state of enjoyment.

The type of pleasure that the self-actualizing people described appeared to be quite different from the usual notion of pleasure, and Maslow derived the idea of peak experience from such descriptions. Such pleasure did not diminish with repetition. It could be described by such terms as awe, wonder, ecstasy, reverence, inspiration, admiration, and so forth. Contrast such pleasures with the usual fun activities of parties, thrills at the amusement park, and the sensuous stimulation at a nightclub.

Other examples of peak experiences are feelings of love; a sense of brotherliness, of the beautiful or of intellectual insights; a nature experience; and religious awareness. These states of altered consciousness are remarkably similar to drug experiences, but, of course, without the side or aftereffects. Those who experience such states of awareness report that they are among the most enjoyable and profound of human experiences. One remembers them as high points in life. Such experiences can be fostered, although not forced, by certain conditions. For example, one can view another person as having a multitude of problems and suffering. One's parents may be viewed as sincere people who are facing difficult problems. One may examine his own life and derive inspiration from the many problems that have been overcome and from the many changes that have transpired throughout the period of growing up. The world is filled with sorrow, suffering, and violence, but it is also replete with miraculous events.

Many people only see the bad in things, and do not tune themselves to the wonders all around them. These are rich sources of peak experiences.

Friendships. Healthy people are capable of intimate friendships, although they usually restrict them to a few. A true friendship requires time and effort, thus one cannot really have many close friends. Healthy people take their friendships seriously and work at them.

Tolerance Toward Others. Tolerance, in this sense, means to accept differences willingly. An intolerant person sets himself up as a standard by which others are evaluated. The self-actualizing people did not discriminate according to age, sex, race, or religious differences. They could relate to and learn from very different people comfortably, a quality which is not common. The qualities of humanness are valued for themselves.

Perception of Difference Between Means and Ends. Several models of personality tell us that those who know what they want and can work to obtain their goals are generally happier and more mature than those who are confused and disorganized. Maslow found that his healthy people had their goals clearly in mind and that they knew exactly what they had to do in order to accomplish them. The means might have to be changed when they were frustrated; but the goals were important enough for them to try to work out a different path toward them. Maslow's healthy people also acted flexibly, and not necessarily according to set cultural standards.

Philosophical Sense of Humor. Most people laugh at the release of hostility, at the downplaying of authority, and at sexual matters; but Maslow's people could find humor in the significant incidents of living, such as discrepancies between what is and what should be. They could laugh at their own shortcomings and peculiarities. For example, one might reread an old term paper and find it to be humorous because of its arrogant tone.

Creativeness. Maslow was fond of comparing the attitudes of his healthy people with the attitudes of a child. He found many parallels, such as a renewed freshness of appreciation of things. He also found creativeness in self-actualizers—not in the sense of great gifts of intellect, but more in the sense of the spontaneity of the child who can become excited about a new way of doing something, or about a new game. Most people seem to lose the fresh naive approach of unspoiled children, Maslow believed. We might think of the excitement of a pet dog when it sees its master coming, the gleeful love play of a couple who care for each other, the sense of exhilaration and freedom of a walk through the woods on a balmy spring day.

Not One of the Herd

It seems that the self-actualizing people are strong-willed, self-sufficient, and strikingly independent of the allurements of the culture. The stereotype of a socialized American does not fit them at all. In fact, they are often considered strange, eccentric, and even antisocial by those who are incapable of appreciating their qualities, or by those who do not take the time to know them. They do not have to impress others by putting on a false front: This is repugnant to their nature. Being basically satisfied with themselves, they do not need the constant reassurance of everyone they meet; thus they appear smug and distant to some people who are threatened by their qualities. Maslow believed that self-actualizing people are less "flattened out," less molded, less dominated by the culture than are average people.

Not Either/Or, But Both. Self-actualizing people have the ability to express opposite qualities in their behavior. They can be both adult and childlike, intellectual and emotional, spontaneous and controlled, serious and playful. Most people make a sharp distinction between such opposites. Of particular difficulty is the expression of opposites at the same time. Can one be playful and working at the same time? For most people it is much more comfortable to be one or the other. We have certain fixed ideas of what constitutes adult behavior—a calm, controlled, unemotional, reasoned approach. Some of the vital qualities, such as spontaneity, freedom to express feelings, playfulness, and so on, must be kept down. Yet these are a part of one's nature and should be expressed. Opposing qualities are often a matter of misperceiving possibilities: One can have long-term goals, but concentrate on the immediate tasks; one can take his life seriously without becoming overwhelmed by failure; one can concentrate on accomplishing goals, but he can also enjoy the means involved in securing them. According to Maslow, so many dichotomies and splits in personality are not desirable. Oppositions in personality are good indications of immaturity.

Being As Selfish As Possible (In the Good Sense)

Maslow advised his students to take seriously the first principle of his brand of humanistic psychology: to be as selfish as possible. His meaning is to take one's life seriously enough to work at it—to make the art of living a major concern. A neurotic takes himself too seriously by exaggerating his problems, but the self-actualizing person considers all the facets of his life important enough to work toward continual improvement. The old admonition that says, "If a job is worth doing, it is worth doing well," applies to the guiding philosophy of a self-actualizing person. He values his work, his time, and himself. By being a more fulfilled person he contributes not only to his own happiness but to others around him and ultimately to society in general. The teacher who is personally involved in his work not only experiences personal satisfaction, but is also a better teacher, as a rule.

Growth-Promoting Activities

A little reflection can provide us with many ways of creating pleasures—reading a good book, learning to pay attention to sensory experiences, even enjoying a well-prepared meal, making friends with our own capacity for thinking and problem-solving, and generally using our creative talents to make our lives more interesting. Many people take friendships for granted and even use their friends to satisfy some of their basic lower needs, but friends can be enjoyed as unlimited sources of stimulation. Maslow once observed that being with nice people actually makes you a better person. Some people are really therapeutic: Their presence exerts a positive effect. You feel better when you are with them. We can all make our lives better through the use of the talents we have.

Dare to Be Great

Maslow often urged his followers to dare to be great, and not to accept mediocrity as a guiding standard. If you put something into life, you have a right to expect a return. Many people believe that they need more lower need gratification—more pleasure, more and better sex, more security, more status and power—but Maslow would point to the highest human needs as the best means of attaining happiness. Following the herd is not the way of the good life for Maslow. One should dare to be himself.

The Productive
Personality:
Erich Fromm

10

Erich Fromm was born in 1900, in Frankfort, Germany. He has a broad background of training and interests. His writings have been influential in sociology, psychology, and psychiatry, and in philosophy and religion. His books are quite popular, both among students and the general public. Fromm is currently living in Mexico City, where he continues to write, lecture, and teach.

Fromm was very much concerned with ideal personality and living. He was impressed with the harmful effects of various social and cultural systems on those who live under the pressures and demands of such systems. Individuals are forced into patterns of behavior and standards of conduct which actually stunt personality growth and block individual potential. Fromm holds that personality can be understood by one's style of life, by what he terms one's orientation to life. The entire personality may become organized around a particular mode of dealing with things, such as a dependent orientation in satisfying needs, meeting obstacles, giving and receiving love, doing work. The ideal personality for Fromm may be described as possessing a productive orientation which involves the active use of abilities and loving human relationships. He also identifies four nonproductive styles of living, and four corresponding nonproductive personality types. The name of each type reveals something of the nature of the personality disturbance. These abnormal types have one thing in common: They look outside themselves for the good things of life.

1. The receptive type develops a style of living which is passive and dependent. Such persons want to be supported and to receive love, rather than doing things for themselves and giving love. They have not outgrown the dependency of childhood.

2. The exploitative type relates to others by using them to get things. Other people are needed, not for what they are but for what they can provide. Even the need for love takes the form of using others for selfish purposes.

3. The hoarding type limits and restricts his involvement. Such individuals build a wall around themselves. They guard their possessions and are suspicious of others. In their love relationships they are jealous and possessive.

4. The marketing type is concerned with making an impression, fitting in, and being considered attractive. In the various aspects of life these persons regard themselves as commodities to be displayed, sold, and compared to others—who are also commodities. Personality is shaped according to the prevailing fashions.

In contrast, the productive type relates to his world by reasoning, by productive skills, and by loving. Through reasoning, he can deal with the problems of existence as a human being. Productive skills create things of real value which produce personal satisfactions. One of these values is love, which gives meaning to one's own life and to those who receive the love.

BASIC CONCEPTS AND PRINCIPLES

Loneliness

Fromm repeatedly stressed the point that everyone feels alone, and especially so in the important decisions of life. We may ask advice from friends, loved ones, and even experts; but in the end, we must make our own decision. How widespread is loneliness? Fromm was convinced that much of our behavior, especially the universal craving for love, was an attempt to overcome loneliness. Many people feel misunderstood—a form of loneliness—even by those who are closest to them. At every major turn in life, from entering school to facing death, we are alone. Fromm saw in everyone a longing for freedom from the control of others, but this freedom produces loneliness because then the person is responsible solely for himself. The college student away from home may feel acutely alone. When the external controls are lessened, one has to be responsible for his own life, but without the familiar and safe protection of external guidelines. This increased freedom may cause a person to seek refuge in drugs, or to join a radical movement in hopes of finding a desired protection.

Relating to the World

Unlike other living things that are governed by instincts, we must relate to our world by knowing and reasoning. Our culture requires much from us; but we do not have instincts to guide us. Furthermore, we are not given a manual of operations to tell us how to live. Whether we like it or not, we are forced into following behaviors and standards that may not at all harmonize with our own preferences, talents, and dispositions. Each person stands alone to work out his own style of life. Traditions can be quite helpful; but even traditions are changing rapidly, and one who clings to them may be branded as an oddity. Fromm believes that no society yet exists that really supports a healthy orientation to life. Our own fosters the marketing orientation that often encourages the development of an artificial personality.

The Five Basic Human Needs

Fromm attempts to analyze what it means to be human; and he comes up with five basic needs that all of us must deal with, whether we like it or not. These needs are a part of our very nature, and if we do not deal with them, we will either die or go insane. Effective living depends on the manner of gratifying the need for relatedness, for rootedness, for transcendence, for a sense of identity, and for a frame of reference that helps to make sense out of our lives.

Relatedness. The profound sense of loneliness we feel can only be alleviated by loving relationships. This means more than romantic love: It means relating to a family, to friends of the same and opposite sex, to children and old people, and, in general, having loving relationships of all types. We need not strive to be the most popular person in town, but we certainly need some human contact, even if it is with a few people. Some people have actually found relatedness through the reverence of heroes and causes, but most of us need more personal involvements.

Rootedness. We need meaningful ties with our environment and the past. Rootedness means feeling a part of something—a job, a home and family, a club, and so on. It is good for us to identify with a set of traditions, even though these are changing rapidly. Lacking rootedness helps to contribute to a sense of being alienated, or the feeling of not belonging. Just as a plant or tree is rooted in the place where it lives, so every person needs to fit in, to be a part of something. This notion is similar to Allport's idea of self-extension, and to Maslow's notion of the need to belong.

Transcendence. This quality refers to a sense of mastery, of control, of being able to solve problems. Our circumstances may cause us to feel helpless and trapped. So many forces control our lives that we may come to feel victimized and powerless. To be dependent and passive is abnormal. A vigorous assertive approach to life in which abilities can be used freely to master circumstances is characteristic of the productive orientation.

Sense of Identity. A sense of identity, according to Fromm, means to have clearly identified roles. These roles are associated with or defined by age, social status, sex, and in general, by the class characteristics that differentiate people. If we are confused about them, our identity is impaired. Usually, the various positions and roles are not clearly spelled out for us; thus many people experience some difficulty with a sense of identity. The people with whom we interact can foster or hinder our need for identity. Generally, being accepted in the various settings that are important to us fosters a sense of identity. Not fitting in engenders a sense of alienation, which, in Fromm's model, means a sense of loneliness and exclusion.

Frame of Reference.   Having a frame of reference means having a set of values and concepts which make life meaningful. It is similar to Allport's notion of directedness or working toward personally relevant goals. We speak of a philosophy of life as one's system of basic values and guiding principles by which one lives, but some people's values and principles are vague and ill-defined. Victor Frankl, the famous humanistic psychiatrist, refers to the seach for meaning, and this comes very close to the sense in which Fromm uses the term frame of reference. In Fromm's view, this is not an extra flourish of living, but an essential requirement, one of our most basic needs.

Man, the Freak of the Universe

Fromm uses a dramatic way of describing the human condition by terming man the freak of the universe. He believes that every one of us has basic contradictions within his nature that create problems which cannot be solved or eliminated. The conflicts within us can reach such intensities that our sanity is tested—at times, to the limit.

What are these awful contradictions in our very nature that we can never completely eliminate? One is the realization that we can never be the perfect person we would like to be. We must live with the desire for perfection and the knowledge that we will not attain it. Another plaguing conflict that we can never escape is the desire for immortality and the knowledge that we will die. We desire justice, but the world is filled with injustice. We can think about the future, but we are not able to control it. We crave to know and make sense of our circumstances, but we must face the awful truth that our knowledge will always be incomplete. We must make binding choices, but usually on the basis of only partial information. We may have a strong need to avoid pain, yet our lives are often filled with it. Fromm believes that the best we can do with these inherent contradictions is to lessen their intensity by developing a productive orientation to life.

Our very nature as a human also creates problems for us, according to Fromm. Everyone can reflect upon his own activities and thoughts. We may not only evaluate what we are doing and thinking, but we may like or dislike ourselves as a result. Our memory is both a help and a hindrance for us: It may plague us with the unpleasant things of the past, but it may also help us to avoid mistakes. Reason helps man to deal with his world effectively; but reason can lead to suspiciousness, to self-deception, and even to the development of the most destructive weapons. Many of our present day ills are the by-product of the use of man's fantastic creative powers.

Human reason keeps man in a state of tension because we are restlessly searching for improvement; we simply cannot accept things as they are. Fromm calls man "the eternal wanderer." One turns to religion; another joins a reform movement; another may even develop neurotic symptoms in his search for improvement.

The person who is driven to achieve wealth, status, and power is also desperately trying to find meaning, no less so than the faithful followers of a religious creed. One of the requirements of being human is the passionate pursuit of something. We simply need something with which to be involved. Whether a person lives productively or not depends upon the types of values which motivate him. The point is that we strive for meaning, whether we know it or not. Obviously, however, if we are aware of our nature, we can use our reasoning powers to fulfill the requirements of that nature. It is every person's lot to find harmony within himself and between himself and the environment. Everyone must make his own world: It is not made for him.

Happiness, a Response of the Total Person

One of the most basic drives is the urge for pleasure and the escape of avoidance of pain. But Fromm holds that many people strive for tension relief and for sensual gratification as the only ways of attaining happiness. Man is capable of the productive use of his abilities; and when these are employed, one experiences the type of pleasure which Fromm holds is happiness. Another facet of man's nature is to love, the expression of which promotes joy and happiness. However, certain pleasures are neurotic, as when a person starved for love relieves his frustration through excessive eating. Some people derive a sadistic pleasure from dominating others. Others may actually derive a perverted pleasure from self-torture. These pleasures are usually followed or accompanied by serious personality and physical disorders. The happy person not only feels happy, but his total organism responds favorably with good health and well-being. An unhappy person, in Fromm's view, shows his unhappiness by a variety of psychological and physical symptoms; both his mind and body may be sick. We can use pleasure as a guide to living, if it results from the productive use of abilities and productive loving.

A father buys his young son a two-wheel bicycle with money that he has earned, not stolen. He buys it because he is proud to participate in the development of his child, not because he wants to relive his own childhood. He gives freely of himself because he loves his son, and not because he wishes to exercise a sadistic control. He experiences joy in helping the child to learn to ride the bicycle because his child is a meaningful part of the father's own life. These satisfactions are not a matter of tension reduction, or sensual gratification; yet they are, for some people, a strong motivating force.

Fromm makes an interesting point about happiness and unhappiness. He believes that it is such a vital aspect of the total organism that even though a person may think he is happy, his body reveals profound unhappiness.

Can Our Conscience Be Our Guide?

We often think of conscience as the little voice within us that tells us what we are doing wrong. But there is much more to conscience. Freud viewed the role of conscience as a kind of watchdog that keeps us in line, makes us experience guilt if we violate certain precepts, and permits us to feel pride if we follow certain ideals of conduct. Fromm sees this type of conscience as abnormal. He calls it the authoritarian conscience, because it reflects principles and standards set by others rather than by the individual. A person who has this type of conscience has not grown up properly. The authoritarian conscience takes the place, within personality, of the external authorities outside of personality.

Those who have power over us can produce in us an authoritarian conscience by rewarding conformity and punishing nonconformity to certain standards. The person takes over these external precepts and judges himself accordingly. Such prescriptions may be unnatural and actually injurious to personality. For example, in several countries in southern Europe, caring for the surviving parent is expected to be the responsibility of the youngest son of the family. In return for support, the parent assists in the duties of the son's household. This arrangement is not necessarily in keeping with the best interests of all the parties involved: It is an arbitrary manner of caring for the elderly. Such obligations are not the basis of a humanistic ethics, but when they are not met, guilt as a result of the authoritarian conscience can be very difficult to cope with.

Fromm believed that it should be possible to establish guides for conduct which are based on the nature of man. Such guides would promote individual development and fulfillment. We can learn about the nature of man in the same way that we can know the nature of anything else, through the use of the scientific method.

The person may be so dominated by dos and don'ts that he does not work out his goals and values. Of course, certain standards of conduct that we have been taught, such as the Golden Rule or the Ten Commandments, are quite compatible with effective living. We should learn the major precepts of the great religions; but, lest we be overcontrolled by them, we should also examine their worth for ourselves.

The most effective type of conscience is what Fromm calls the humanistic conscience. It is our loving care for ourselves. The humanistic conscience is a rational response to living. We know that certain things are good and that other things are bad for us. For example, a person who drinks to intoxication may violate certain codes of ethics, but from the standpoint of humanistic conscience, he is commiting the sin of self-abuse. One violates his humanistic conscience when one limits his growth and functioning, or when one injures himself.

The Meaning of Sin in Humanistic Ethics

One of the meanings of sin is the falling short of a target. One commits sin in a humanistic sense when he misses the mark; thus sin means the misuse of abilities, or the squandering of talents, or self-injury. A person violates his own best interests and lives less effectively than he might. Sins of omission are quite as significant as sins of commission. Any harmful habit is a sin in humanistic ethics because it hinders growth and fulfillment. Even failure to try to use one's abilities fully is sinful, if one thinks of one's goal as becoming all that one can be.

ABNORMAL TYPES

In the process of growing up we have many lessons to learn, and earlier pleasures and ways of doing things must be given up. As we have noted, Fromm holds that a total orientation to life may be formed as a result of difficulty with one of the major lessons of living. The total character of the person reflects this failure in living. A particular cluster of traits is developed for each of the nonproductive orientations. For example, a person who deals with his problems in a passive or dependent manner has a number of defining traits; and the same is true of the other nonproductive orientations. Successful accomplishment of the major lessons of living fosters the development of useful traits, and these support a productive orientation to living. Stubbornness is an exaggeration of a desirable trait—the necessity to pursue actively what we desire or need.

The Receptive Orientation

Many people organize their total personality and living around a dependent and expectant mode of dealing with things, rather than working for what they desire, or giving of themselves in a social relationship. Such persons lack initiative, and expect others to provide for their needs. Often this type of person limits his needs and consequently develops a pessimistic outlook on life. The person accepts his lot as inevitable and resigns himself to a low level of existence. His sense of personal pride is weak because he must submit to others in order to live in a dependent relationship. Self-confidence is low, and the person may be described as spine-less and cowardly. The receptive type may also lack shrewdness. He has a sentimental view of love, and expects to fall in love with an exciting ideal. The receptive personality desires love desperately as a solution to all problems; but actually he is a poor partner in any type of human relationship because he is unwilling or unable to give love in the active sense that Fromm speaks of it.

The Exploitative Orientation

An active orientation to life involves interacting with other people in a give and take manner; but the exploitative orientation is one sided: Other people are used. Often the person is self-centered and selfish in his relationships. A pleasant social person-ality often hides the manipulative drive. The person uses social skills to get what he wants. In relationships with the other sex, he is also exploitative. He may be quite seductive, but this is only a means to get what he wants out of a love relationship. He may initiate a love relationship in order to prove his charm, but he may be attracted most by those who are already attached. In his view, human attachments are simply a means to satisfy his own needs; they do not involve mutual love.

The Hoarding Orientation

Effective living requires that we learn to hold on to what we have, as a protection from those who might exploit us. Saving for the future for unexpected emergencies, or simply to get the things that we want is one of the most important lessons of living. Failure to learn this lesson is reflected in such traits as unimaginative conformity, stinginess, and suspicion of others. The hoarding type may be cold and detached in social relationships. His orientation to life may be also highly conservative—even apathetic and lethargic. Others find him dull and uninspiring because he follows fixed paths and routines. He may be superintellectual and unemotional. The love relationships of the hoarding type are characterized by possessiveness and jealousy.

The Marketing Orientation

Fromm was very much impressed by the artificial approach to life that is fostered by a capitalistic society such as ours. He held that capitalism promoted the marketing orientation. For many people, the major concern is to impress others. One's worth as a person is externally based because it is determined by others: "I am as you want me" is a guiding ideal of the marketing orientation. It represents an exaggeration of social concerns.

One of the undesirable traits of the marketing orientation is the inability to be alone. The person with a marketing orientation does not like to be alone for very long. It appears that he is afraid to look at himself, and that he needs constant social contacts, probably as a means of support, because what determines his self-worth is external to himself. He may have difficulty staying with anything long enough to meet his objectives. In social relationships and business, he is sometimes quite tactless and offensive in his zeal to attain status. He is undiscriminating about getting support or attention from others: He wants to make an impression on everyone. Although he is always seeking social contacts, he can be quite insensitive and indifferent to the feelings of others. He is very much caught up in the latest fashions. In the extreme form, the marketing type lacks any real loyalty; and he may drop a commitment, even to a friend, for the sake of a better deal or prospect. The marketing type may actually lack principles and values; he may exist strictly for his own gain. He does not care who gets hurt, so long as he comes out on top.

It should be noted that there are some people who nearly seem to fit one or another of these nonproductive orientations exactly; these are less common than the mixed types. For one thing, the traits may vary in degree, and not all the traits of a particular orientation may be found in an individual. Furthermore, traits of several nonproductive orientations may characterize and mingle in a particular individual. In general, these orientations are either exaggerations or deficiencies of normal traits. The productive orientation is actually made up of the same traits as the nonproductive orientation, but they appear in a moderate degree, or, in the case of the negative traits, in their opposite form.

IDEAL PERSONALITY IN LIVING

The Productive Orientation

We might think of each of the nonproductive orientations as a failure in acquiring the traits of effective living. As a person develops and broadens his encounters, new traits are required, and each adds something significant to personality. The traits must exist in just the proper balance, so that they support each other. This is an ideal which is never fully achieved by anyone.

One of these traits is to be receptive to others, accepting certain inevitable conditions without undue frustration and resentment. Relationships with others require faithfulness and responsiveness. One should be able to be modest and charming to others, while maintaining self-respect. To be adaptable and socially adjusted is an ideal of living. The normal receptive person knows how to live with other people because he is sensitive to their needs. He is optimistic, polite, trusting, and tender towards others. These positive traits, which seem to have their origin in the earliest years of life, are certainly essential for a productive orientation.

Being active in dealing with one's circumstances promotes effective living. There are certain traits that promote an active approach rather than exploitation. Consider the trait of self-assertion: Standing up for one's rights and making valid claims are essential requirements of living that must be done properly. One should be able to follow his own impulses and enjoy self-confidence, even in the face of repeated failures.

Although a person need not be a miser, certain traits do promote a better future. Being practical, economical, and careful in money matters is essential for living effectively in a complex society such as ours. One must learn to regulate what he wants according to his resources. Certain other traits, such as being patient and reserved, help one to work effectively toward his goals. A person must learn to be cautious and steadfast in his pursuit of ends. One should be calm under stress, and be able to work out and follow plans. In social relationships one should be capable of loyalty.

In a real sense, we do have to sell ourselves. We must compete for status, grades, marital prospects, and for practically everything else. We have considered the abnormal traits of the marketing orientation: The following are the same traits in desirable form. One must learn to make himself physically and socially attractive. One should strive to maintain a youthful attitude toward life supported by curiosity and willingness to try new things. Work is to be taken seriously, and one must be able to adapt readily to new situations. Openness and tolerance in dealings with others is necessary to productive living. We ought to live comfortably with our fellow man, without trying to make everyone conform to our images of people. We might strive to make ourselves enjoyable to be with. We generally like people who are forward-looking and optimistic about the future.

As we have noted, the ability to love is essential to a productive orientation. Loving relationships are not only enjoyable because they give expression to vital human powers, but also because through loving contacts everyone relieves his terrible sense of aloneness. Fromm believes that we must cultivate the art of loving as an important part of the art of living.

The Role of Love in Life

The ability to reach out and become involved with other people is one of the most intriguing qualities of man. Many people never get enough love and human warmth. They feel isolated and unlovable. One can hardly listen to popular songs, turn on the television, attend a movie or play, or read a magazine story without running into the theme of unfulfilled love. Love is such an important part of our lives that we can expect to have difficulties with it. Here, we are using the term "love" in its broadest sense, as Fromm does, to encompass all forms of human attachments with other humans. Any major personality disturbance will be reflected in some problems with love. One or more of the aspects of loving may suffer: for example, one may dominate his loved one rather than allowing the person to be himself; one may demand more than one is willing to give; or one may dictate terms and conditions for giving love rather than accepting the person as he is.

Many people believe that love is something that happens to a person when the appropriate love object is present. We "fall" in love. But Fromm believes that true love is an active process, and that it is a quality one cultivates through practice; thus one becomes a loving person through the practice of loving behaviors. A loving personality is something to achieve. Fromm uses the term love in a manner considered, by some people, to mean intense liking.

A number of highly emotional states are falsely identified as love, in Fromm's view. These include infatuation, physical attraction, sexual stimulation, and romantic involvement. We do sometimes meet someone of the opposite sex who fascinates us. We may become captivated by certain features of appearance, by a manner of laughing and speaking, and by personality traits that are especially appealing to us. Sexual attractiveness also adds to the infatuation; but Fromm does not consider these attachments as love. These are things that happen to a person, and they may be a prelude to the formation of a loving relationship.

True love, whether motherly, brotherly, or erotic, or whether it means loving one's parents involves four qualities: care, respect, responsibility, and knowledge. Without these qualities the attachment is something other than love, in Fromm's opinion.

Care means an active concern for the loved one, rather than simply being concerned about one's own feelings. Responsibility means responding to the needs of the other in a giving way. Respect means to accept the person, without setting conditions or trying to change the other individual. Knowledge means really striving to understand the person—from *his* point of view and perspective.

Portrait of the Productive Person

Fromm's ideal personality is highly complex, possessing all of the traits of the various orientations to living in a moderate and balanced degree. He resembles Freud's ideal personality in that social values are emphasized. Civic concerns are also important: Devotion to family and being a loyal and productive worker are valued. Fromm's ideal person has lessened the conflicts within himself and between himself and society; but his orientation to life goes far beyond compromise and self-limitation. It is a life in which the distinctively human qualities are developed fully, and expressed with joy and happiness. The productive person is similar to Allport's mature personality—quiet, forceful, warm, loving, sociable, inwardly directed, and working toward becoming highly productive.

BEHAVIORISTIC MODELS: LEARNING AND BEHAVING MAN

IV

We have considered several models of personality which have one common theme: They are based on the assumption that personality is a "something" whose structures and operating principles can be known and depicted by concepts and principles. We have been introduced to active psychic agents or processes such as traits, needs, instincts, intentions, dispositions, and so on; and to a variety of dynamic factors such as the pleasure and reality principles, the principle of reinforcement, self-actualization, and striving for superiority and security. We have also indicated that although the inventor of a particular model bases his concepts and principles upon his actual observation of behavior, or perhaps upon his own experiences, the behavior is assumed to be caused by agents within the personality. When Freud speaks of the id, he really means to refer to instincts and basic drives that are a fundamental feature of the personality.

When Allport refers to a central trait, he is saying that there is something within the core of the personality which actually influences behavior. Situations are interpreted according to the nature of such traits. Those who hold that personality comes between the environment and behavior maintain that once we know the nature of personality, we are in a much better position to relate behavior to its causes because personality itself is a major source of the causes of behavior.

It seemed to many that a bright new day began in psychology when early in the development of American psychology John B. Watson proposed the daring idea that psychology should dispense with the psyche. This view came to be called "the empty organism" approach to man because it considered only observable behavior, and not the unobservables that were supposed to exist in the personality. Watson argued that we could obtain solid and dependable knowledge about man through observing what a person does in different situations. If music is introduced into a work setting, we can easily record the changes in behavior without trying to get into the personality of the workers. We can measure production output, the amount of waste, the amount of time spent at the drinking fountain, and so on. It would be quite difficult to determine whether the workers feel better or like their jobs better with music playing; but anyone can observe the changes in behavior and behavior outputs.

Furthermore, Watson perceived that an outstanding thing about man is learning, making new responses to the various situations of life. People can be taught effective habits and skills that are useful. Watson actually proposed that he could take an average child and make of him whatever was specified: a genius or a dullard, a productive member of the community or a criminal. The learning history of the individual makes all the difference in the type of person one becomes. It was a bright new program for psychology which offered a great deal of hope for mankind as well. Currently, B. F. Skinner is making many of the same claims. Agreeing with Watson, Skinner proposes that human behavior can be engineered, not by trying to influence minds or change personalities, but by changing the environment. Skinner is particularly concerned with the control of behavior which is possible through the use of rewards. He argues that we can control behavior by controlling what follows behavior: its consequences. Skinner has been primarily concerned with the professional modifier who shapes the behavior of others; but many of his concepts are applicable to the control of our own behavior, and we will focus on this aspect of behavior modification in Chapter 11.

Some current psychologists who also call themselves behaviorists believe that the empty organism model is inadequate. They accept the idea that important personality determinants exist; but they have redefined the traditional personality factors in behavioristic terms such as: self-talk, expectancies, perceptual responses, cognitive sets, and the like. Although the value of these redefinitions of the traditional personality factors remains to be determined, many behaviorists are using these concepts as a basis for changing behavior. We will also consider the potential value of such approaches in dealing with our own self-management efforts. In Chapter 12, we will consider the potential for self-management through mind control as interpreted in the light of these new behavioristic models.

Self-Management Through Behavior Modification: J. B. Watson, B. F. Skinner

11

The advancement of science has produced a vast accumulation of knowledge about material and living things in our world. The mysteries of the nature of man have also been the object of study for centuries, first by philosophers and theologians, and then by the various branches of science. In the hands of the philosophers and theologians, the pursuit of knowledge was primarily for its own sake. This was exemplified by the Greek scholars who were concerned with making sense out of the world. The desire to control natural events was so powerful that even in this ancient period there were priests and witch doctors who attempted to predict and influence the course of nature. But as dependable knowledge increased in scope, the picture changed. Knowledge is now used increasingly for practical ends. Principles of physics are applied to real problems through mechanics, engineering, and electronics. Biological principles are used to improve the breeding of animals and plants, to grow edible food, and for a host of other useful purposes. The amazing developments in chemistry are being translated into new plastics, drugs, and other benefits for man. As knowledge of man's nature increased, there was also the impetus to use that knowledge to improve man's conditions of living. This spirit of applying knowledge was best exemplified in psychology by the behaviorists who sought to make psychology as objective as any of the natural sciences.

In this chapter and the next we will consider the thinking of several outstanding behaviorists. The name behaviorism was originally applied to those who stressed the study of observable behavior rather than psychic states. The so-called stimulus-response behaviorists directed their attention to the relationship between a particular stimulus (e.g., a loud sound) and an observable response (e.g., a startled reaction). They viewed man as being primarily a reactor to the stimuli of the environment—sights, sounds, odors, people, events, and so forth. For them, the psyche consisted of response tendencies that could only be set off by stimuli. I. P. Pavlov, the famous Russian physiologist who pioneered research in the conditioned reflex, and J. B. Watson, the famous American founder of behaviorism, were both impressed with this approach to the study of human nature.

Although there is no question that we are constantly reacting to this or that stimulus or stimulation, it is equally valid to point out that man is a doer, an actor, an inventor, and a builder. We act upon the environment, as anyone can readily perceive by looking all around him. We are always bringing about change in our world. The world is as much man-made as it is natural. The natural effects or consequences of our own behavior will influence that same behavior. We observe the consequences of our own behavior; and we either continue with that behavior or change it— if it turns out to receive punishment. E. L. Thorndike, the famous educator and early pioneer in animal psychology, and B. F. Skinner, who is the most outstanding behaviorist today, stressed both man's *behavior* and the *results* of behavior. Skinner has developed a whole new technology of behavior control by manipulating the outcomes of behavior: That is, he has discovered techniques for modifying and controlling behavior which involve the systematic use of rewards. In addition to rewards, painful stimuli and punishment have also been used by other behavior modifiers.

The four behaviorists noted above have attempted to understand human behavior in terms of observable stimuli, responses, and the products of behavior. They have avoided concepts and principles that assume the existence of an active unconscious mind or psyche. However, several current students of man who also call themselves behaviorists, or more precisely, cognitive behaviorists, maintain that we cannot dispense with an active psyche. They are also interested in controlling behavior; but they hold that this can be accomplished most completely by taking into account perception, cognition, problem solving, and decision-making—factors which are usually considered faculties of the mind. It seems quite evident to them that humans can perceive, think, plan, judge, and make decisions irrespective of the immediate external stimuli. Even behavior which is primarily under the control of an external stimulus is really more directly caused by one's perception of the meaning of the stimulus. For example, the value of money is interpreted differently by people from different economic classes.

Just as our interpretation of the people and events in our environment is quite personal, so also is our interpretation of the products or consequences of our own behavior. What one person considers a rewarding effect, another may consider as punishing. We always bring into a situation a past history of perceptions, expectations, values, and emotional tendencies. These personality factors will determine both the meaning of the stimuli we encounter and the meaning of the consequences of our behavior. The cognitive behaviorists hold that our knowledge and ability to influence behavior would be incomplete without consideration of these personality variables. These ideas are advocated by such behaviorists as A. Bandura, A. Ellis, J. Rotter, J. Dollard, and N. Miller and will be discussed in Chapter 12.

CONTROLLING CAUSES
AND CONSEQUENCES OF BEHAVIOR

The Value of Self-Management

If you visited one of our giant corporations, you would be impressed with the coordinated activities of thousands of workers running hundreds of complicated machines. The final product is the result of the thinking, planning, and harmonious working together of many specialists who make their contribution to one or more aspects of the various projects. Each person must be capable of managing his own life and circumstances in order to contribute to his company. Often, there is a long period of sustained training, followed by an apprenticeship, and then years of experience on the job. All these activities require a high degree of self-control and self-management.

Self-management cuts across practically everything we do. Many people struggle along with much less than they could get from life because they are incapable of accomplishing what they set out to do. The things that count most for us usually demand a high level of self-management. It is becoming clear that self-management techniques can be learned. We can apply the same analytic approach to self-management behavior as is being used with other types of behavior study. We already know about learning to break useless habits, ridding ourselves of irrational fears and sensitivities, suppressing obsessive thoughts; but more importantly, we know how to acquire useful skills and achieve our long-term goals.

Conspicuous failures in the art of self-management may be found in prisons and in mental hospitals; but many of us who are considered normal really fail to achieve the fulfillment of our potential. While self-management is held up as an ideal in our society, most people do not get very far with this important aspect of living. Which of us does not have one or more bad habits, sensitivities, useless worries? How many people can really follow through with their plans?

One person struggles a lifetime with an overweight problem,

and encounters repeated failures. Another person cannot control his drinking habit. Still another cannot quit smoking. Another person finds himself getting tense in social situations, and avoids them as much as possible. How much better would our lives be without these unwanted habits? We can also look at self-management from the standpoint of desirable habits and skills. Most people appreciate the value of daily exercise and other health-promoting measures, but how many can actually get themselves to do them? How many people fail at school or at work because they cannot work independently? How many people fail to stand up for themselves because they cannot be assertive enough to fulfill their own needs?

Self-Management and Goals

One of man's greatest assets is the capacity to think about and work for the future. We can set goals for ourselves and work diligently to achieve them; or, more correctly, the person who is capable of self-management can. We have both long-term and short-term goals; but most people are caught up with their immediate goals—getting rid of momentary tensions, satisfying needs and drives, relieving boredom through recreation, and even making something exciting happen. When we strive toward a goal, we experience some tension. But short-term goals usually create much more tension than do long-term goals. For example, eating is much more important to a hungry student than is the term paper due at the end of the semester. But then, so are relaxation and recreation for many students. A person may have many desirable long-term goals, but his short-term goals always seem to take priority. One essential feature of self-management is to somehow increase the tension of the long-term goals. One way to do this is to divide long-term goal into many subgoals. These various subgoals become the target behaviors—reducing smoking by five cigarettes a day, cutting out a hundred calories a day, getting started on the term paper by developing a set of note cards, and so forth. The point is that each target goal should be rather easy to achieve, as one moves gradually, step-by-step, toward his final objective.

Self-Observation and Self-Monitoring

A condition for self-management is self-observation or self-monitoring. Frequently this may be painful. One might begin by observing nonthreatening behaviors for developing skill in self-monitoring. Gradually, one might focus on the undesirable habits. Sometimes it is necessary to monitor not only our own behavior, but also that of others; thus one who wishes to become more assertive in social situations should monitor the reactions which result from attempts to be assertive.

Recording Behaviors

In order to undertake a program of self-management, one might begin by specifying the behaviors that are to be changed. The change might be the reduction of the frequency, intensity, or time of an undesirable habit. Recording may be done by a counter, a note pad, or any other inconspicuous device. Whether one counts calories consumed, cigarettes smoked, instances of complaining or submissive behavior, it is useful to have an indication of the present strength of a habit. Any changes that occur can be easily noted. Focus on the changes can serve as motivation to continue the self-management program; but also, as several studies have demonstrated, the sheer act of recording behavior is a good way of initiating the process of change. One who wishes to cut down his drinking may be assisted by simply keeping track of the amount of drinking. Although recording behavior in and of itself does not produce significant and enduring changes, it is beneficial during the initial period of a self-management program in helping a person experience easy successes.

Behavior Change Through Intense Desire

The common sense notion about self-management is that it is simply a matter of will power or strong desire. This view holds that if you want something bad enough, you will find a way to get it.

The old adage tells us "Where there is a will, there is a way." This idea highlights an important principle of self-management: that in order to attain self-management, one must be strongly motivated, and must make a commitment to change. The best self-management program in the world will lead to naught if the person does not apply it. The desire to change may be strengthened by thinking about the undesirable consequences of the bad habit, and also about the good effects that change will produce. This type of thinking is also a good means of resisting the temptation to perform the undesirable habit.

The desire to change, no matter how intense, does not guarantee that a person will take the right steps, as many would testify who have tried sincerely and repeatedly to break a bad habit. We might use the analogy of a person trying to lift a heavy object by brute force alone. The object might be more than he could lift, however intense his desire; but if he used the lever and fulcrum device, or a block and tackle, the desire could be translated into successful achievement. In the same way, the desire to change is a good prerequisite for putting self-management techniques to work.

Controlling and Controlled Behaviors

A particular behavior may be controlled by another behavior: For example, eating ice cream is controlled by purchasing it at an earlier time. The buying of the ice cream is the controlling behavior with respect to the eating behavior. A particular undesirable behavior may be the last link in an entire chain. We often make the mistake of trying to control the actual undesirable behavior at a time when the desire is quite intense and the object is quite available. It may be almost impossible to resist eating the ice cream, once it is in the freezer. The desire for the ice cream was much less intense when it was purchased. It would have been a lot easier to resist it then. Self-management is often best achieved by working directly on the controlling behaviors: not buying the fattening food, limiting the amount of money for lunch, avoiding certain places and situations which favor the bad habit.

Controlling the Environment

We have repeatedly mentioned that immediate setting, circumstances, and stimuli influence our behavior to a remarkable degree. Habits become so automatic that they act like reflexes: In the presence of certain stimuli they are set off in machine-like precision. In some situations, the ability to control behaviors is greatly diminished or nonexistent. Until we break the connection between the stimulus and the response, we remain a victim of the habit. One excellent method of controlling behavior is to control the stimuli which activate it. We certainly have the ability to alter our physical and social environment. We can take the path to the library rather than that to the snack bar. One can limit or determine the kind of food which he purchases. One may bank a certain amount of money when he gets paid, irrespective of any obligations, and make do with what is left.

In arranging a study routine, a student might determine which situations and conditions interfere with studying behavior—reading while lying in bed, the presence of the newspaper or of unanswered letters, and so forth. On the other hand, those stimuli which favor studying can be substituted: having a set place and time for studying, taking easy preliminary steps such as quick reviews of chapters, keeping necessary material near at hand, preparing the desk with pleasant objects such as flowers, pictures, quiet music, and so forth.

In our own daily activities we can observe our reactions in specific situations with a view to changing both the situations and the responses. We are constantly reacting to stimuli. Our emotions are frequently stirred up by the situations and people we encounter. Self-knowledge and self-management can be improved by knowing the situations which are significant for us. There are numerous ways in which we can alter our environment to foster better living. Many of our problems are due to the immediate stresses: We may lose interest in our friends, dislike the job we are doing, or feel trapped by our present circumstances; but new friends can be found, jobs can be changed, and even immediate circumstances can be altered by moving to a new place. Thus we should carefully consider the potential for self-management which is possible through altering our environment. We must remember, however, that changing the environment does not solve the problem if the problem is within ourselves.

The Role of the Consequences of Our Behavior

We have the capacity to change some aspects of our environment, and we can work to gain ever more control of environmental forces. Also, our behavior produces effects which we can observe, and on the basis of which we can make further adjustments. The natural effects or consequences of our own behavior may be either rewarding or punishing. A student who attempts to fraternize with his teacher may elicit in her a negative response, and this may cause the student to hold back on his spontaneous reactions and expressions in the presence of all teachers.

It is possible for one who has control over another's circumstances and life to "engineer" a program of behavior modification, as B. F. Skinner convincingly demonstrates. Thus, the behavior modifier might determine (1) the specific behavior he wishes to build or shape; (2) the types of rewards for the specific individual; (3) how the rewards are to be given. In the early stages, in order to stimulate behavior, rewards are given for even approximations of the correct response; but gradually, more and more of the correct behavior is required in order to earn the reward. There is no reason that we cannot establish our own behavior modification program. If a student is having difficulty with studying, he may work out a series of goals to be achieved, making certain that the environmental stimuli which instigate competing behaviors are eliminated. He identifies certain rewards that he can use as incentives for study behavior. He works at it gradually by rewarding himself for increasing study time a small amount, and so forth. As strange as it seems, this procedure, if carried out effectively, really does work, even though the rewards have no intrinsic connection with the studying behavior. The reward must be made to follow the specific achievement: for example, drinking a cup of coffee when the chapter is read. As skills improve, one may gain positive natural effects, so that the rewarding procedure may be dropped. Good study habits become automatic and under the control of certain cues.

Self-Rewarding and Self-Punishing

The reader may devise numerous ways of rewarding or punishing his own behaviors. One may work out a series of rewards which vary in desirability. One may even follow the professional behavior modifiers and use tokens which can be translated into tangible rewards. In general, it seems to work out better to reward specific behaviors rather frequently. An author may be able to get his work out rapidly by setting weekly goals for himself, and then by breaking these into daily tasks. By setting a goal, one establishes a standard of performance, and failure to achieve it may cause guilt. In order to avoid guilt, our author must meet his quota for the week. Self-rewarding and self-punishing are ultimately individual matters, and one should work out his own system through trial and error.

Self-Management Through Mind Control: A. Ellis, J. Rotter, A. Bandura

12

If we wanted to help a person change his behavior, we might investigate what that person thinks about in certain critical situations. We would probably find that his reactions and behaviors, normal or abnormal, would be the result of what he thinks about the situation. This assessment of a situation, in turn, depends upon some basic beliefs. If it happens that such beliefs are faulty, the person's thinking and behavior would be maladaptive. The behavior modifier would argue that the disturbed behavior is the most concrete aspect of the total response, so we, or the person himself, ought to attempt to modify it directly; but those who stress mental causes would argue that the behavior is the last link in the chain. We, or the individual himself, should modify the thinking and even the assumptions or beliefs behind the thinking, as the best way to bring about a change in behavior. A person who believes that his bad moods should be easily controlled may engage in much self-criticism, but the fact is that often our moods are based on natural rhythms of the body, over which we have little control.

Self-Instruction in Positive Self-Talk

If we examine our psychological reactions in troublesome situations, we will find that we often instruct ourselves in negative ways. We may say things such as: "I can't take an essay test"; "I really do not have much to contribute that others would like to hear"; "I am not the type of person that people like." These self-verbalizations have been so frequently repeated in similar situations that they occur like any other well-practiced habit, mechanically and automatically. We may not even be aware, until we deliberately focus attention on this type of thinking, that it occurs at all. What is necessary to change our reactions and behaviors in the same situations is to interfere with these automatic habits. We can substitute self-supporting and self-rewarding thoughts. A person may tell himself to move slowly, to keep things under control, to take one step at a time, and so on. These positive statements should be practiced in relatively neutral situations at first. Once such statements become habitual, the person should deliberately try to say them to himself in more stressful situations.

Pertinent here is the correct appraisal of events. It is helpful to gain the proper perspective about a painful experience by comparing it to other painful experiences of both greater or lesser severity. The intensity will often diminish as one sees the event in a broader frame of reference. This procedure also helps us to interfere with the automatic hurt reaction, which can, initially, be quite intense. Once a habit of reappraisal can be established, it will be automatically invoked in painful situations.

Controlling Negative Emotions Through Correct Thinking

Albert Ellis has stressed the power of correct thinking as a means of controlling our emotions. As we noted previously, we are constantly confronted with emotional situations, and often it seems that our emotions have the upper hand in our lives. Ellis points out that our emotions depend upon our knowledge, and that knowledge may be based more upon our interpretation of reality than upon reality itself.

Why Do We Misperceive and Misinterpret?   We all want to know truth and face reality, yet misperceptions and misinterpretations are everyday experiences in all our lives. What accounts for this apparent contradiction? Many situations and events are difficult to understand because they are complex, or because we simply have not had previous experiences with them. Furthermore, we may have to deal with inconsistencies and contradictions: Even good friends occasionally hurt our feelings; parents, teachers, and supervisors are not always what they should be; justice does not always prevail, and so forth. Our thinking is muddled because the events themselves are confusing. Is the unpleasant situation due to our misperception of it, or is it simply an unpleasant reality of life? Although we are strongly motivated to see things as they are, we are also motivated to preserve our self-esteem and to avoid pain. These motives are even more powerful than the wish to be in touch with reality; thus, under their influence, we may distort, deny, and use the defense mechanisms that Freud delineated. One other significant cause of reality distortion, as we mentioned previously, is our false beliefs and assumptions. Here we are reminded of Horney's "claims" and "shoulds."

What We Tell Ourselves.   Many emotional experiences are caused by our own self-talk, what we tell ourselves about the things that are happening. The actual event is interpreted in an exaggerated way. A young man is turned down by a girl whom he asked for a date. He may begin to tell himself many unflattering things: "It was an awful experience; I am not like other guys; I really don't seem to get along with anyone very well; no one really likes me." He has activated some very unpleasant emotions by his own self-talk. It may turn out that most of what he tells himself is false; but the fact is that he believes what he tells himself, and his emotions are real enough. The emotions are the same, whether the person fits the description or whether he simply believes that he does.

Emotions and Self-Talk.   We might further examine the nature of an emotion to see the connection between knowledge and feeling. Strong emotions involve complex organic processes of the body. We experience some of these, such as accelerated heartbeat, breathing changes, tightening of muscles, drying of the mouth, and cold hands and feet. This state of arousal becomes a part of the current psychological context. In other words, the particular emotion we experience depends upon what we are thinking and telling ourselves. A person who is about to take a test usually experiences some emotional arousal; but if he begins to tell himself some unpleasant things about failing, about his personal inferiorities, and so forth, what began as a mild anxiety becomes an emotional upheaval. To prevent this, one must say the right things, as we noted earlier.

Compounding Sentences.   To return to the example of the young man who was turned down for a date, Ellis would describe his internal verbal behavior as compounding sentences, by which he means elaborating an experience by making false statements about self. Although it is true that he was turned down for a date, it is not true that the young lady criticized him, or told him that he was inferior, unlovable, or anything else.

Drawing Invalid Conclusions.   Another way to look at compound sentences is from the standpoint of faulty logic. In our effort to obtain an undistorted picture of events, we often go too far and actually draw invalid conclusions from real events. The young lady did refuse the date, an unpleasant fact of life, perhaps, but that is all she did. The experience might have been interpreted quite differently, with much less emotional upset: For example, one should expect some failures in dating; no one gets everything he wants; it only takes one other person to make a successful marriage, and so forth.

Irrational Thinking

A person may be so caught up in his problems that he makes frequent errors in reasoning about them. As we have noted, irrational thinking can be habitual and automatic. Being alert to some typical errors in reasoning can help us to avoid them.

Overgeneralization. A common error in thinking is to overgeneralize from single instances. We may conclude, on the basis of a particularly painful mistake, that we are a failure. If we have acted stupidly in a situation, we may overgeneralize, and conclude that we are stupid. The logician would tell us that we are drawing unwarranted conclusions on the basis of a single occurrence. The psychologist might point out that failure is a part of the business of living. A person who does many things exposes himself to failures; and one should learn from them, and then forget about them as soon as possible. Behind the exaggerated reaction to failure is the unrecognized belief that one should always be a winner and experience no pain.

Either-Or Thinking. Another common error in thinking is to split things one way or another. If you are not faithful in everything, then you are faithful in nothing. Either the world has to be perfect, or else it is worthless. Just because a college education is not good for everyone, then it is not good for anyone. It would be much easier to deal with things if they were clear and unambiguous, but this is seldom the case. There are degrees of truth, of desirability, of justice. We all behave inconsistently and irrationally some of the time, and perhaps we can deal more effectively with ourselves and our world if we keep in mind some of the pitfalls in thinking.

Interpretation Rather Than Description. It seems that we are always placing a value on things, people, and events. This was a good day, or a terrible experience; I like this person better than that one; my instructor really put me down in class this morning. It seems desirable, at times, simply to resist making a value judgment and just to accept facts as they are. A blue-collar worker might say something like, "I am only a laborer." His statement expresses an interpretation rather than a description.

Unrecognized Internal Sentences

We are often troubled by our own behavior because we do not understand it. A man may be having a great deal of friction with his wife, but he may not know why, nor may he be capable of controlling his negative emotions toward her. His unrecognized internal sentence may be, "My wife treats me like a child." A strong habit of not being openly critical of his wife may actually block the full awareness of this internal sentence. As we have noted, we often react automatically without really taking account of what we are saying to ourselves at the time. A student may feel miserable because he does not receive all As. His unrecognized assumption is that only As are acceptable. Unrecognized internal sentences hinder self-management because one is under the influence of a false guiding principle. Even if his unrecognized sentences are correct, without awareness of them, the person is operating with only partial evidence. Unexplained emotional reactions are frequently due to such unrecognized internal sentences.

Behavior Management Through Redefining

We can lessen the impact of a painful experience by taking a second look, and then by redefining it. We might be quite upset about the loss of time and money involved in repairing a dented fender; but when taken in proper perspective, it is a relatively minor event. We will have to accept and deal with numerous such instances. After one's emotions have subsided, one should review the disturbing experience and try to view it from an outsider's frame of reference. We cannot undo what has happened, but we certainly can obtain a balanced view of it.

Even relatively neutral events are subject to individual interpretation. Is the bottle of wine half full or half empty? One student exclaims that there is only ten minutes left before the bell, so there's not much point in starting anything. Another student looks at the same situation quite differently: For him there are ten minutes more, during which time he can get something finished. Surely, the significant events of our life are worth reappraisal.

ROTTER'S SOCIAL LEARNING MODEL

We can promote self-management through any one or a combination of the following: changing our perception of events, changing our expectancies, changing the value we place on goals, or changing the disordered behavior directly through controlling environmental stimuli and the effects of our own behavior. We have already examined several of these alternatives; we will take up the others as J. Rotter, who is viewed as a cognitive learning psychologist, sees them.

We Learn Expectancies

Our experiences teach us to expect certain things to occur in specific situations. When an expectancy is firmly established, we are set to interpret things in a certain way. Some of our most important expectancies are taught by highly respected authorities—parents, teachers, ministers, television stars, heroes in books and magazines, and so forth. One of the most tragic things about our expectancies is that they are false, overglamorized, and totally impractical. We are simply deluded by the important people in our lives in regard to every aspect of life. Children's stories usually have a happy ending: Everyone gets his due, and the good guys always win out. We are dazzled by beautiful love stories, by happy family living, by the great joy of holidays, and so forth. Life is difficult enough without striving for the unattainable. Under the influence of false expectancies, one experiences frustrations and dissatisfactions even when circumstances are quite favorable. Everyone experiences sorrow, disappointment, failure, unfaithful friends, accidents, and struggle. All of these remind us of the existential problems of being human. Yet many people have expectancies that do not include such unpleasantries.

The circumstances of life change for us: We must all face the facts of aging, of friends and loved ones who die, or move away. Many people have highly idealistic expectations of love, sex, marriage, and career. Even in religion, we may expect the wrong things—perpetual peace and well-being, a clear conscience and purposeful guidance, and a tension-free life. Unfortunately, such expectations are often the result of promises which are made by those we admire and respect; thus we accept them without questioning. Because such promises encompass highly prized values, we eagerly accept them. If such wonderful things are possible, who would want anything less? But of course, no one really lives the way the models are portrayed. It seems that we spend the first half of life learning false expectations, and the second half moderating them.

Expectancies Limit Freedom of Movement

Rotter points out an important aspect of expectancies, our freedom of movement. A strong expectation of failure will limit one's initiative: "What's the use of trying, if I usually fail." The person has a general set, or disposition, to fail, so he protects himself by not trying. If this set could somehow be changed to an expectation of success, the total picture would be quite different. The person then has a much greater freedom of movement. Many people report that they feel ill at ease and uncomfortable in social situations, or in dealing with a stranger. Rotter could point out that they do not feel free to be themselves because they have expectancies of saying the wrong thing, acting stupidly, making a mistake, and so forth. These expectancies are carry-overs from their past, when they might have been criticized by parents or teachers for speaking freely. If we experience a great deal of restriction and fear, we should look to our expectancies because they determine our freedom of movement, whether it be broad or narrow.

Expectancies May Generalize

Generalization means that we respond in the same way to a whole class of things and people. Bad experiences may produce an expectancy that generalizes to a whole class. Prejudice is a striking example. One who has an expectancy of rejection by members of the opposite sex brings this to every new social relationship; and the contact may result in the support of the expectancy because we often make our expectancies come true.

Expectancies Are Influenced by Value of Goals

In order to understand behavior, we should not only know expectancies but we should also know the amount of value which is placed on the goal of the expectancy. If one values something very much (e.g., high job status) even if his expectancy of success is low, behavior will be directed toward the attainment of this goal. Under the influence of highly valued goals, many people strive vainly for glamorous goals. The value of the goal is the only consideration for some people; thus they vainly pursue unattainable goals, or accept as desirable only certain high standards of achievement. Rotter terms this condition high minimum goal level. When a person says something like, "I can only be happy if I graduate with honors, or if I become a physician, or if I have a perfect marital partner," we have instances of high minimum goal levels. We can see that self-management can be promoted by examining our expectancies, the value we place on our goals, and the standards that we consider acceptable. All of these can be highly unrealistic.

OBSERVATIONAL LEARNING

Success in self-management is not possible without observational learning. This type of learning is also called modelling by Albert Bandura, who is the leading investigator in this field. We learn many things from observing people we admire and respect. The child identifies with parents and teachers and copies their behavior and values. Children will also imitate the behaviors of other children, or the leader of their crowd. Adolescents copy the hair styles and dress of sport stars and other glamorized models. We all have someone that we look up to and attempt to copy. Sometimes we do it deliberately, but at other times it is unconscious. The tendency varies in intensity from person to person, but it is quite strong in most of us; thus the type of model we choose is extremely important. One way of learning roles is through observing others, but if there are inappropriate models, or none at all, important adaptive behavior may be lacking. We have pointed out that we learn from the natural consequences of our own behavior; but relying exclusively on such "natural" teachers can lead to many mistakes and unnecessary pain. Successful adaptive behavior is not always consistently followed by rewards, even when those rewards are contrived. We can learn to perform successful behavior simply by observing successful people. Furthermore, we can avoid many costly mistakes by observing the behavior of the right models. The type of model we select is an important factor. As we have noted, the art of living is not formally taught, but certainly one of the most vital ways of acquiring it is to observe those who are successful. Often people fail because they do not sense what is expected of them. The aspiring young executive may be overly aggressive, argumentative, negativistic, and so forth in attempting to demonstrate his leadership abilities; and though he doesn't know it, his behavior is offensive. Having a model to imitate can be extremely useful in learning the correct behaviors. Self-management is, in part, determined by our images and ideas; thus the nature of those images and ideas is an important factor to be considered.

Conclusion:
Personality Models
in Practical Perspective

13

WHAT TO DO WITH THE MODELS OF PERSONALITY

The best way to conclude this survey of the models of personality is to reread the first chapter to see whether the objectives
stated there now make more sense. Speaking of rereading, the
models contain concepts and principles which are universal and
timeless. They will have a different meaning at different periods of
your life. Personal application and interpretation of the concepts
and principles may be a continuing venture—and, perhaps, a
rewarding adventure for you. Had you read these models five
years ago, they would have had a different meaning; and as you
re-examine them at different times in the future, they will be
interpreted from the frame of reference of a different life style.

The models will only be useful if their component concepts and
principles are personalized by observing specific behaviors in

ourselves and others. The concepts and principles are abstractions, but they were derived from actual observations of behaviors. They can only acquire meaning for us if they are applied to specific behaviors. For example, we know that Freud intended the term superego to include behaviors pertaining to "musts" and "oughts." Each person has a superego, and its nature is unique to that individual. No one else has the exact same standards of conduct, sense of guilt, and so forth. As we have noted, Freud pointed out that the nature of the superego changes with the development of personality. It makes a real difference whether the superego remains fixated at the stage of childhood. An adult who has a child's superego is immature. Furthermore, if the superego does not become an integral part of the ego, the person will experience unexplained guilt, depression, or a sense of unworthiness. The point is that we will better appreciate the changing nature of the superego if we know the behaviors that define it; and this point applies to all components of the models.

PERSONAL APPLICATION
OF MODELS OF PERSONALITY

We have already noted that knowledge of many models of personality can broaden our own models, and thereby increase the scope of our understanding of people and of our selves. We can then make sense of more behavior and comprehend the wide differences among the various people we encounter. Furthermore, the potential causes of our behavior should be more evident to us; and of course, with knowledge of the causes of our behavior, we are in a better position to change it.

It seems valid to propose the hypothesis that a particular model of personality describes and explains the behavior of some people better than others. Freud based his model, as did all the others, on his observations of his disturbed patients. We are all familiar with the notion that often people resemble each other in appearance, or have similar speech patterns. We may extend this idea further to include personality itself: People may fit into a particular life style or have a similar personality make-up. Take the matter of dealing with frustration: Some people react by withdrawal; others by attacking the source of the frustration; and still others by some type of compromise. Most people can be described by one of these reactions. Students of human nature have been typing people for centuries—extrovert-introvert; the short, fat, jolly person versus the tall, slender, shy person; people who move toward, away from, and against people; and so forth. Thus there must be some basis for typing them. If we accept the hypothesis that each of the various models applies to a specific type, it would be possible to identify the one that best describes and explains you. You can gain insights about yourself from studying the model, just as an architect might study a drawing to get a picture of the layout of a house.

Each model tends to specify an outstanding problem and also suggests what should be done to overcome or remedy it. If a sense of inferiority is a problem that is especially acute for you, you should become more acquainted with Adler's model because he has stressed this factor more than any other. If loneliness is especially painful for you, you might look to the model proposed by Erich Fromm, who had the most to say about it. If conflicts threaten to tear you apart, Freud might be consulted. The models are presented rather briefly in this book; but you may, at least, be able to identify the model that best suits you. The next step is to read an account by a disciple of the model, rather than going directly to the original source. Finally, you may attempt to read an overview of the model as presented by its originator.

MODELS LEAD TO ACTION

Our own models have a profound influence over our total behavior. The model we have of the child makes a real difference in our thinking, feelings, and expectations of what is normal or abnormal behavior. A person who views a child according to adult standards (as being an inferior adult) will impose many restrictions, demand strict conformity to codes of behavior, and, in general, exercise a great deal of authority in "running" the child's life. On the other hand, if we view the child as a growing person who has an inherent right to be himself, we will behave very differently: Our approach might be much more permissive and democratic.

The traditional model of women has greatly limited the roles which are considered acceptable for women. Many people view women only in terms of the roles of homemaker and mother. What is acceptable and unacceptable behavior for women is changing because the model of women is undergoing change.

It should be quite apparent that our models are not academic curiosities, but, rather, that they exert a powerful influence over our behavior. What we consider normal or abnormal behavior for various groups and ages depends on the models we have of them. Maslow has pointed out that all our institutions are based on the model of man as being basically evil. Child-rearing practices, our entire educational system, current policies and practices in business and industry, and even religions and ethics assume that we need constant threats of punishment, strict control and monitoring, ever-present discipline, and a strict and punitive conscience. His own model stresses individual freedom and spontaneous expression.

The recognition that we carry around various models of people should itself draw our attention to the necessity of our becoming more aware of their nature. Awareness of them increases our potential to change—to change our behavior by working directly on changing the models themselves.

WHAT IS THE GOOD LIFE?

There are many formulas, recipes, and creeds that tell us how to live the good life. The ancient Romans would counsel us to live fully each day by indulging our drives and appetites: "Eat, drink, and be merry, for tomorrow we die." Many theologians would find this rather limited at best, and quite degrading to man at worst. They would advise us that the good life is an adequate preparation for the next life; but many people today want something more from their lives than a trial. Within some religions, there are humanistic influences that seek to promote a better life here on earth, while preparing for the next life.

The models we have considered have given us a variety of answers to our question about the good life. One tells us to seek a conflict-free life, with a strong ego that is socialized. Another tells us to find loving relationships with people, and to work productively at something worthwhile. Another looks to our highest needs as being especially important in living effectively and fully. Another model tells us to develop all aspects of our nature as fully as possible. Are these various approaches simply different ways of saying the same thing? Perhaps, but some of them are contradictory. Could it be a matter of emphasis? Again, each model seems to focus on a specific problem area and to offer a single comprehensive solution based on that problem area. Here again, we are encountering the matter of individual differences. We would agree with Allport's view that there is no one right way to live. It is inconceivable that the extrovert or the introvert, the highly intelligent or the mentally retarded, could follow the same goals—unless these are stated in such general terms as to be meaningless.

The life style proposed by Rogers fits some people, but so do the ones proposed by Allport, Freud, Jung, and the others. Find the one or the combination of a few that appears to fit your nature and aspirations, and use it as a guide to living.

Suggested Readings

ADLER, A. *Practice and Theory of Individual Psychology.* New York: Harcourt, Brace, and World, 1927.

ADLER, A. *Problems of Neurosis.* London: Kegan Paul, 1929.

ADLER, A. *Social Interest.* New York: G. P. Putnam's Sons, 1939.

ALLPORT, G. W. *Personality: A Psychological Interpretation.* New York: Holt, Rinehart and Winston, 1937.

ALLPORT, G. W. *Becoming.* New Haven: Yale University Press, 1955.

ALLPORT, G. W. *Pattern and Growth in Personality.* New York: Holt, Rinehart and Winston, 1961.

BANDURA, A. and R. H. WALTERS. *Social Learning and Personality Development.* New York: Holt, Rinehart and Winston, 1963.

DOLLARD, J. and N. E. MILLER. *Personality and Psychotherapy.* New York: McGraw-Hill, 1950.

ELLIS, A. *Reason and Emotion in Psychotherapy.* New York: Lyle Stuart Press, 1962.

ERIKSON, E. H. *Childhood and Society,* 2nd ed. New York: W. W. Norton and Company, 1963.

ERIKSON, E. H. *Identity: Youth and Crisis.* New York: W. W. Norton and Company, 1968.

FREUD, S. *The Standard Edition of the Complete Psychological Works.* London: Hogarth Press, 1963.

The Psychopathology of Everyday Life, 1901. Vol. 6

Introductory Lectures on Psychoanalysis, 1917. Vol. 15-16.

Civilization and its Discontents, 1930. Vol. 21.

Outline of Psychoanalysis, 1938. Vol. 23.

FROMM, E. *Man for Himself.* New York: Holt, Rinehart and Winston, 1947.

FROMM, E. *The Sane Society.* New York: Holt, Rinehart and Winston, 1955.

FROMM, E. *The Art of Loving.* New York: Harper and Row, 1956.

FROMM, E. *The Crisis of Psychoanalysis.* New York: Holt, Rinehart and Winston, 1970.

HORNEY, K. *The Neurotic Personality of Our Time.* New York: W. W. Norton and Company, 1937.

HORNEY, K. *Our Inner Conflicts.* New York: W. W. Norton and Company, 1945.

HORNEY, K. *Neurosis and Human Growth.* New York: W. W. Norton and Company, 1950.

JUNG, C. G. *Psychological Types.* New York: Harcourt, Brace, and World, 1933.

JUNG, C. G. "The Archetypes and the Collective Unconscious," *Collected Works,* Vol. 9, Part I. New York: Pantheon Books, 1959.

JUNG, C. G. *Man and His Symbols.* New York: Doubleday and Company, 1964.

MASLOW, A. H. *Toward a Psychology of Being,* 2nd Ed. Princeton: Van Nostrand, 1968.

MASLOW, A. H. *Motivation and Personality,* 2nd Ed. New York: Harper and Row, 1970.

MASLOW, A. H. *The Farther Reaches of Human Nature.* New York: Viking Press, 1971.

MILLER, N. E. and J. DOLLARD. *Social Learning and Imitation.* New Haven: Yale University Press, 1941.

ROGERS, C. R. *Counseling and Psychotherapy.* Boston: Houghton Mifflin, 1942.

ROGERS, C. R. *Client-Centered Therapy.* Boston: Houghton Mifflin, 1951.

ROGERS, C. R. *On Becoming a Person.* Boston: Houghton Mifflin, 1961.

ROTTER, J. B. *Social Learning and Clinical Psychology.* Englewood Cliffs, New Jersey: Prentice-Hall, 1954.

SKINNER, B. F. *The Behavior of Organisms.* New York: Appleton-Century-Crofts, 1938.

SKINNER, B. F. *Walden Two.* New York: The Macmillan Company, 1948.

SKINNER, B. F. *Science and Human Behavior.* New York: The Macmillan Company, 1953.

SKINNER, B. F. *Beyond Freedom and Dignity.* New York: Alfred A. Knopf, 1971.

SKINNER, B. F. *Understanding Behaviorism.* New York: Alfred A. Knopf, 1973.

THORNDIKE, E. L. *Human Learning.* New York: Appleton, 1931.

WATSON, J. B. *Behavior: An Introduction to Comparative Psychology.* New York: Holt, 1914.

Index